BEYOND
YOUR DOORS

Strategies that Breed
Community Transformation

Dr. LaVerne Adams

Beyond Your Doors

ISBN 978-0-9848567-8-7

To all of my students
that I have taught over the years
all over the world
about what it means to be strategic
and authentic "change agents".
May we ever be
about our Father's Business
seeking always to make
a dynamic difference in the world.
I celebrate you.

Acknowledgments

I distinctly remember the defining moment that I received the phone call from Ian Scott, who was the director of the Eastern School of Christian Ministry at Palmer Theological Seminary in 1998. He called to tell me that he had heard about the great community-focused work that I was doing in our neighborhood and wondered if I could teach it at the seminary to church leaders because I was the "expert". "Expert," I wondered? I didn't know that anyone even noticed that I was simply serving my community in a way that met a felt need. I totally unaware, at the time, that doing this kind of work would make me an expert. But it didn't take long for me to realize why this was the case once I began teaching. There were many well meaning people who wanted to help their community but so few people actually doing it. If it had not been for that phone call I am not sure what direction my life would have taken.

Very recently, in a meeting with church leaders from around the country my Bishop, David Evans, from the Abundant Harvest Fellowship of Churches, introduced me as an expert at community-focused ministry and stated that we have a "genius" in the room. Needless to say I was shaken by this labeling and so I asked him in the most humble way that I could, "Why did you say such things about me?" His emphatic response was what shifted my understanding about myself and who I am in the Body of Christ and the world: "Because I've seen it!" If I had not figured it out by now, his words solidified my calling and my conviction to help others, help others.

An expert is a specialist; an authority who has a professional and proficient way of understanding an area or assignment and knows the best way to get the job done. A genius is a mastermind who uses the intellect and can see on a deep level how things work together in the world. Looking at these definitions, I can honestly say that I embrace both as how I go about my work to help transform the quality of people's lives. Oftentimes, we cannot see what is best within ourselves. We need others to help us to understand who we are and how we are to make an impact on the world.

I will also never forget the day that Rev. Dr. Wilson Goode, former mayor of the City of Philadelphia, supported me in a meeting with grantors for a literacy program. I spoke up about the overbearing requirements that were being placed upon us as grass-roots organizations which were far more than we had the capability and funding to handle. He told the funders around the table "You'll better listen to that lady, she is saying what everyone else around this table is thinking." Needless to say when he offered to coach me in my community-focused efforts, I was elated. Although I had been performing in this work for many years, he had always been an integral part of our work. But I was becoming frustrated about the lack of resources available to do so. He provided the insights and support that I needed to forge forward.

It was Maya Angelou who said, "The first time someone shows you who they are, believe them." But the converse of this is also true. The first time someone shows you who 'you' are, believe them." This is especially true when the person on the other end of the tribute is a person of integrity. I have discovered that what they are giving you are the clues to your destiny in life.

Because I have come to the place to be truly in touch with who I am, I understand that I am uniquely altruistic. Therefore, I acknowledge and celebrate these and the many other persons who have encouraged me with their confidence in my abilities. What I do for others is the greatest gift that life can have. For it is only in giving that you are truly living.

Foreword

For the past 50 years as a churchman, community activist, and political leader and now as a senior statesman, I have sought to bring about both transformation of lives and communities. In 2000, I concluded my doctoral studies focusing on congregation transformation with a desertion titled "From Clubhouse to Lighthouse", a dialogical approach to Congregation Transformation – my interest in Transformation of Congregations and communities has increased since 2000.

Dr. LaVerne Adams in this book has expanded the landscape of knowledge and strategies for the role of the church in community transformation. She makes it clear that the central role of the church is beyond the doors and walls of the edifice.

For those who are scholars of the Bible, there is little doubt that Jesus wants His church to extend beyond the building we worship in. He wants it to be more than a Clubhouse for members. He wants it to be a Lighthouse. The problem is that tradition in many churches is that of a Clubhouse church; a church of the members, by the members and for the members.

Dr. Adams challenges us to reach beyond tradition and embrace the whole Gospel of Jesus for the whole world. She not only issues the challenge but she lays out a strategic agenda to take the church from where it is now to where it needs to be now. And it is supported by the Word.

Dr. Adams shows that those who love God and want to serve Him will honor the Gospel not by following man-made rules but by following biblical mandates.

The strategies outlined in this book are a roadmap to congregational and community transformation. And if these strategies are followed, they can take local churches from Clubhouses to Lighthouses.

Dr. W. Wilson Goode, Sr.
Senior Fellow, Public/Private Ventures
Distinguished Senior Resident Fellow, Fox School-
University of Pennsylvania
National Director, Amachi

Contents

INTRODUCTION

I am very passionate about helping to improve the quality of people's lives individually, socially and globally. It is what makes me feel the most alive. After teaching for twelve years in the seminary, to hundreds and even thousands of church leaders, I believed that it was time to make a shift. Although it was extremely rewarding, I desired to make a greater impact on persons other than those that attended the traditional institutions of higher learning. This material is for anyone who wants to make a real difference in the world by reaching out in a meaningful way to their community. It is designed to be learner-focused. The intention is to help Christian individuals and congregations discover the link between their calling to be both preachers and doers of the Word, in a hurting and broken world. The goal is for us to examine how personal passion, congregational connection and community transformation are related and should be leveraged through practical holistic ministry and social service.

This book highlights the direct relationship between the local church and her community. The reader will explore the relationship between the biblical mission of the Church and the important process of social change. Biblical patterns will be compared with historical examples. We will look at several contemporary models of Christian service that have brought about significant community change through visionary leadership, local community outreach and a focus on mission.

The aim here is to enable church and community by providing them with a theological frame of reference to help them to make the biblical and intellectual choices needed to take strategic action. The objective is to help congregations to be better equipped when involved in the work of the church to intentionally do ministry beyond its doors. It is rare but important that leaders are given an opportunity to share particular aspects of their unique calling to community-focused ministry with others. This is vitally important for hands on learning, as well as an opportunity for feedback before launching out. The Community-Focused ministry draft is that opportunity to strategically create a work that is effective and sustainable. It is presented in a format that can be shared with others.

The material contained within this book is designed to help the reader to be able to:

1. Identify Old and New Testament foundations relevant to the biblical ethics of doing ministry beyond the doors of the church;

2. Utilize a theological frame of reference and think critically about how local mission work relates to improving existing social processes;

3. Analyze ministry styles that would contribute to the positive influence in community through faith-based ministry;

4. Compare historical and contemporary cases of Christian churches and community organizations in the active process of social transformation;

5. Understand the necessity to cooperate and collaborate with others to bring about effective community-focused ministry;

6. Discover elements necessary to effectively execute a community-focused ministry;

7. Have a renewed sense of the urgency needed when relating the gospel to the church and community-focused ministry;

8. Organize and effectively implement a community-focused ministry; Evaluate and critique community outreach efforts for effectiveness.

Before us we have the tremendous opportunity to make an enormous contribution to our communities and ultimately the world. It is my hope that as I reach more people than those who have already been touched by this material in the classroom, millions will be touched with the message of personal, social, and global transformation. You hold within your hands the tools to begin the process. Jesus promised to be with us always even to the end of the age. The Holy Spirit was given to us to lead us and guide us into all truth. Regardless of where w are, we have all of the resources that we need to get started. Let's follow the example of Christ, be about our Father's Business, and go beyond our doors!

Strategically yours,
Dr. LaVerne Adams

PART I

LOCKED INSIDE THE DOORS

CHAPTER 1

"What is The True Mission of The Church?"

While you are reading this chapter, you may want to reflect on your role in the church and what you will personally do to make a difference in the community.

When considering community-focused ministry, it is critical to ask the question: What is the true mission of the Church? In today's post Christian society, there are many who are hostile against the church. The reasons may vary but oftentimes the Church is in a romance with itself and has a difficult time looking beyond its narcissistic lover to see the real object of affection: the community. When we think of it this way we can understand the hostility of the world because it primarily feels neglected and is crying out for attention.

Christ sacrificed his life to save a dying world. Sometimes when we look inside the doors of the church, there is hardly a resemblance of this. When we are self-centered as a church, we are in direct opposition to the life of Christ because Jesus was selfless. When we were dead in our sins, we were the object of His affection. This resulted in his sacrificial act of giving because he loved us so much he did not want us to have to pay the penalties for our own sins. As Christians, we should follow the example of Christ and become servants of the Kingdom of God by offering selfless service. As we appreciate what God has done for us to transform our condition, we should become change agents in our society.

A reason why this could be virtually impossible for the individuals in the church building is because they themselves have not been truly transformed and therefore they cannot give what they truly do not have. This is why the bible makes it so clear how it is possible to be hearers of the word and not doers of the word[1]. When we understand this limitation, the only remedy is that we "…be not conformed to this world: but be ye transformed by the renewing of your mind, that ye may prove what is that good, and acceptable, and perfect, will of God."[2]

After teaching community-focused ministry for over a decade, it became more and more clear to me that there

---

[1] James 1:22
[2] Romans 12:2

are many people who go to church who have no clue about why the Church exists. Some believe that it exists only for the sole purpose of serving and meeting their own personal needs. Others feel like the church is like Burger King: a place for them to get things "their way". Then there are others who have a "membership mentality" who feel as though the church is a place of status, privilege, and entitlement. And so if there is a sense of ambiguity with those who are members within a congregation, is there any wonder that those outside of the church question its purpose?

If you were to ask the question of what is the true mission of the church, you would get answers like: "The church

"…is supposed to witness."
"…should be teaching God's word."
"…should be doing evangelism."
"…should be in unity."
"…should be a place of worship."
"…should be a place of service."
"…should be a place of healing."
"…should be a place of prayer."
"…should be a place of love."

These are some of the responses that I have received in my classroom. And the list goes on and on. I am sure that you would agree that all of these answers are right but more often than not we miss the mark. There are apparent reasons why this is the case. Somehow members get distracted with their own personal issues. The real problem with the church is that it is filled with imperfect people. We are fully consumed with what makes us imperfect and therefore are unable to stay focused on the true mission of the church.

It is not so much that the people are wrong as much as it is that they are oftentimes weak. But it is to these same weak, imperfect people that have been given the mandate to serve a perfect God in a hopeless world. And it is in our human imperfection that we come to the table sometimes with hidden agendas. These hidden agendas take center stage and personal issues become the focus. This is what sometimes causes the church to be self-centered and even selfish at times. This becomes apparent through some denominational divisions and differences of opinions. The clash in belief systems causes an ethos of "rightness" which becomes more important than "righteousness." The pathological syndrome of "we are the only ones going to heaven" stems from "we are right and everyone else is wrong." This kind of is small-minded "stinking thinking" suffers from amnesia regarding the command to go to are people in the world who are desperate to hear of the saving power of Christ.

Then there is the worldliness that creeps into the church because there are those who lack the spiritual disciplines and therefore do not possess the spiritual strength to stand against it. Because they practice their faith with such inconsistency and irregularity, there is no telling where the world ends and the church begins. Consequently, the true mission of the church is left unfulfilled, held hostage to another agenda of worldly demands because no one wants to "rock the boat".

To make matters worse, those who have tenured membership in a church feel as though they are entitled to get whatever they want and believe that the church would not function without them. The sensitivity to the gospel is overruled by the power struggles and politicking often found in churches that have lost their way.

In addition, many churches have lost their vision of why they exist and as a result are perishing day by day. Commercialism has also crept into the church making it virtually impossible to remain spiritual as it relates to stewardship. What churches do to survive would not be considered acceptable to even civic organizations. But as the church gives in to the pressure of these unwholesome attitudes, it resembles that of an ingrown toenail – painful and potentially dangerous. This is precisely what prevents the church from fulfilling its mission to the community. It is in pain from its own self-inflicted wounds and is potentially dangerous to anyone who comes in contact with it.

But there is hope! There are ways to turn around even the most wayward congregation and help nurse it back to spiritual health so that it can regain a sense of purpose. But first, we must honest with ourselves. We have to look critically at where we are if we are going to see the necessity for the much needed changes in our churches. We are going to have to explore some of the ways that we moved away from our mission. Then we are going to have to take the risk to incorporate corrective measures into the corporate life of the church as well as explore opportunities for modifications. Ways to see a dynamic shift begins with an intentional attitude adjustment of the people within the congregation to willingly submit to a transformational process. Here are some initial recommendations for members of congregations:

- The church can be spiritually energized through corporate prayer and fasting;
- Corporate study is another great way to revive a church and move it from its deadly perspectives;
- The members of the church should practice unconditional love for one another and learn to appreciate their difference and their diversity as God's grace on display;
- Selflessness is critical and flexibility is vital if a church is going to function in unity;
- They should avoid at all costs destructive criticism of any kind. There is just NO place for it in

the Church of God. Only satan is the accuser of the brethren.[3]

A godly focus should be placed upon the commonalities rather than the differences. It will take every effort to model Christ-like behaviors but it is worthwhile work if we are willing to fulfill the mission of what we are called to do as a body of believers.

When we are intentional to embrace change as individuals, then and only then can we even attempt to embody change as a congregation. And when we experience change in the congregation, then we are prepared to go out and make a difference in the world. Building relationships within our walls is a great place to start, if in fact, we are going to interact with others within the communities beyond our doors. It is vitally important that we build nurturing relationships within the congregation and then model those behaviors outside within society. And I am confident that with a little effort, we can do this.

When the conditions of our neighborhoods are less than desirable, the church needs to take the risk necessary by first being truly converted and then doing what it takes to see a conversion in the community. It is therefore critical that the church model what they hope the world to be by activating the principles that we are called to live

---

[3] Revelation 12:10

by. Those in the church who claim the Lordship of Christ should truly let him be the Lord of the "ship". This should create the synergistic transformation that is needed in our world. But we must first realize that it takes work for us to become change agents in our society but the process will effectively produce a visible difference in community.

And we should not be afraid to let our "mess be our message" and our "misery to become our ministry". In this respect we exhibit our real authenticity. Then we are in a better position to share the same grace, love and acceptance that we were given to everyone we come in contact with. This is how we can expect to see a total transformation in our neighborhoods because we have moved beyond the doors of our churches into the places that God has called us to go providing the caring, compassionate embrace that a loving God wants to give. When we actually behave the way God intended, we gain the awesome ability to exemplify the characteristics of an awesome God to a confused and hurting world.

This may sound audacious but it is completely possible because we are only talking about starting with just one small area or one community at a time. This is important given the statistics that almost 60% of Protestant churches in America have a membership of less than 100 persons. In addition, 35% of churches have a membership of under 500. That is a whopping 95% of all churches having a membership of fewer than 500 persons.[4] I don't believe that God is more pleased with big churches than God is with more intimate congregations. These statistics prove that regardless of the size of the church, it already has what it takes to accomplish the goal of community transformation – a mandate from God to "go out into all the world."[5] What I do believe that God is looking for is quality over quantity. It is what you do with what you have that matters. After all, Jesus used only 12 people to turn the whole world upside down!

Furthermore, when we look at the life of Jesus, he singlehandedly infiltrated the preexisting religious and social conditions. Although he was a king, he was not standoffish from the pain and nor did he remove himself from the ugliness of life. Rather he directly involved himself with people regardless of their station in life. He understood them, their culture, and customs because he positioned himself as one among them. He talked to them on their level. He introduced the new concept that they could now be in relationship with God as their father. They had never heard of such a thing. God as Creator, yes! They understood this. But to have the ability to have an intimate relationship with God?... That

---

[4] Hartford Institute for Religious
search. http://hirr.hartsem.edu/research/fastfacts/fast_facts.html#siz
econg
[5] Matthew 28:19

was unheard of. Needless to say, Jesus embodied this and was considered a radical. In spite of the opposition, he knew what his mission was and he let nothing get in his way.

In order to make a difference, like Jesus, we need to be the difference. Regardless of what stands in our way, we should be here to help people to become free from the things that plague them in life. But this is not possible if we ourselves are not free. We must be aware that Christ is available to us to help us, help others. This is the true mission of the Church. We do not have to do this alone.

BEYOND YOUR DOORS MINISTRY ACTIVATION

While you were reading this chapter, how do you feel your role in the church has advanced or hindered the mission of community-focused ministry?

What are you destined to do with your life? Why are you here?

What are you doing with your gifts, talents and abilities that could make a positive difference in the world?

What corporate or secular jobs do you hold or have you had that can be translated into Kingdom work? (Many Christians overlook these valuable assets)

What is your plan to use these areas in your community-focused ministry?

What is God asking you to do to make a difference?

What is your plan for the salvation of your community?

CHAPTER 2

A Biblical Frame of Reference for Community-Focused Ministry

As you read this chapter, think about what ways the Church can fulfill its Kingdom Mandate to do community-focused ministry.

There is a story about a woman who receives a letter in her mailbox from Jesus that I read to my students in class. In the letter, he tells her that on that day, he would like meet her for lunch. In wonderment, she is concerned why the Lord would want to meet her. Excited, she begins to vigorously clean her house. She only has a few dollars until payday but grabs her coat and rushes out to the store to buy the best meal that her money can buy. On her way back, she notices a couple in the alleyway near her home. They ask her for food. She hesitates because she has bought food for her special guest but the man tells her that he has been living on the streets and has no job and they haven't eaten. He also explains that his wife is cold and pregnant. The woman begins to make an excuse but feels the familiar twinge in her heart. Before she knew it, she handed over all of her food and her coat. She just couldn't help herself. Although they were appreciative, now she is in a pickle. She is having her special guest and had nothing to serve and she is worried. As she entered her home, she notices another letter in her mailbox. This was odd because she had already received her mail that day. When she opened the letter she found these words: It was good to see you again. Thanks for the lovely meal and beautiful coat. Love always, Jesus.

I can hardly keep from tearing every time I read this letter aloud. Here we see more than just a moral code of ethics. Ethics can be defined as a system of moral values as we remember what our mother taught us or principles in what grandma said. Every society has a "golden rule". But this becomes even more important when you are a called a Christian. Our ethics of accountability, compassion and empathy are foundational to our belief system and they should shape our behaviors and who we are as a people. What happens in the story is based upon foundational principles that we are mandated to live by. This is not optional nor out of convenience but should prick our conscience with conviction.

A passage of scripture that I believe can be helpful in demonstrating the Kingdom mandate of the Church can be found in the exegesis of Matthew 25:31-46 and should dynamically affect our conscience as it relates to community-focused ministry. It is expressed as follows:

> *"When the Son of man shall come in his glory, and all the holy angels with him, then shall he sit upon the throne of his glory:*

At first glance of this scripture reference, we have to make the obvious inquiry of "What time is it in the Kingdom of God?" The answer is clear to many but the reason for asking the question may not. Most would say the Great White Throne Judgment, and they would be eschatologically correct. We can consider this as the ultimate moment in time and the fulfillment of all things when Jesus returns. But what is extremely significant at this very critical time is that it deserves our undivided attention because it is what takes place at this time that serves as an instructional premise for providing community-focused ministry.

> *"And before him shall be gathered all nations: and he shall separate them one from another, as a shepherd divideth [his] sheep from the goats:*[6]

---

[6] Matthew 25:32

Now that we have an idea of what time it is in the Kingdom of God, we need to also have an understanding about who is present. We see from the text that the Son of Man is there in the seat of power in all of his glory. His position seated on a throne signifies his authority to rule. His holy angels are there too acting as attendants. All nations are present and represented but we have to wonder: Who is "not" there? If in fact it is the time that we have deduced, then "everyone" whoever was and ever will be is there because all simply means "all." It is vitally important for us to note this because there are no exceptions here.

Oftentimes when we are not willing to hear the gospel, we think that the message is for everybody else. In this particular case there seems to be no one left out. There are no other options. Every nation is just that: every nation. Everyone is required to be present because at this time, there is no place else to be. This is significant because here we see a direct overruling of the will. We will soon see why because we can assume that there are those who may not care to be in this moment...

"And he shall set the sheep on his right hand, but the goats on the left."

It is clear that the King has the power to rule and he is exercising his authority as he orders a separation. But are there really animals in heaven? of course not! The book of Revelation is filled with imagery and symbolic language. What we are being made aware of is that it all boils down to two distinct character types that will be judged based upon their behaviors. Some have the characteristics of sheep while others have behaved like goats. Both are being judged based upon their works that resulted from their nature. It is important that we get the symbolism here because they are apparently separated based upon these traits alone. The right side is indicative of righteousness. The sheep, who are often considered dumb, meek, mild, easy to lead, timid, and fearful are sent to the right side. This is odd because the world teaches us to behave just the opposite to get ahead and now we see that the lifestyles that represent the more aggressive behaviors ultimately do not pay off in the end.

It is the soft, gentle, vulnerable, submissive, peaceful, dependent, trusting individuals that end up on the right side. What is remarkable is that it is in a sheep's nature to require leadership or else they will go in circles with a herd-like mentality. Therefore it is easy to assume that they have these types of behaviors because they were led to be that way. They obviously submitted to a process and hence they have produced these results. What is even more interesting is that they were willing to be led and so as a result they received the pre-planned benefits of the leader. The text suggests that these benefits were prepared for these types of people from before the foundation of the world. Therefore it is assumed that it is the nature and characteristics of these people who willingly submitted that get the blessing. Using this criterion alone, we can predict who will be separated on the left sent into eternal punishment and damnation, and who will be invited to be blessed with the everlasting inheritance of the Father.

> *"Then shall the King say unto them on his right hand, Come, ye blessed of my Father, inherit the kingdom prepared for you from the foundation of the world:*

First exhibited were the character traits of the people who were invited to go to the right hand. Next, we see the unique activities that produce the results of getting sent to the right side. It is the description of these activities that gives us clues about what we should be doing and what it takes to receive the reward of a blessed inheritance. At first examination, these things seem small in comparison to the great reward. But it would behoove us to take note that we are called to meet even the most basic need. And as simple as this sounds, it is consistently doing the little things that makes the greatest impact on our society.

> *"For I was an hungred, and ye gave me meat: I was thirsty, and ye gave me drink: I was a stranger, and ye took me in:*
>
> *Naked, and ye clothed me: I was sick, and ye visited me: I was in prison, and ye came unto me."*

What is amazing here is that now these "sheep-like creatures are considered righteous because they have displayed what Jesus considered righteous acts. They are sent to the right side and they reap a righteous reward. But what is even more amazing is that they didn't even seem to realize that the power of what they were doing it. This is clear from the text because they are taken by surprise that such small heartfelt gestures are seen as great acts with such phenomenal rewards. We see that the recipient of these good deeds is obviously indiscriminant. So much so that the righteous ones don't even realize who it was directed toward…hence the line of questioning:

> *"Then shall the righteous answer him, saying, Lord, when saw we thee an hungred, and fed [thee]? or thirsty, and gave [thee] drink?*

> *"When saw we thee a stranger, and took [thee] in? or naked, and clothed [thee]?*

> *"Or when saw we thee sick, or in prison, and came unto thee?"*

Now the response…

> *"And the King shall answer and say unto them, Verily I say unto you, Inasmuch as ye have done [it] unto one of the least of these my brethren, ye have done [it] unto me."*

Jesus is the King. And the King is making it very clear that even the least of these is important to him. And shouldn't they be important to us as well? Jesus proves that not only is he is very interested in being everywhere, and in every thing but also in every one. Because the language of the text is housed in the imagery of characteristics and traits, we need to dig deeper to explore exactly what this text is saying to us today. In doing so, we can better understand the ministry Jesus is passionate about us providing.

If we look closer we find that these can be summarized into four categories: feeding, hospitality, clothing, and visitation. Food and drink are vital to our natural survival and Jesus knows this. Sometimes we can be so callously spiritual-minded that we can be no earthly good. How can we witness to someone who we know is hungry, or cold, or hurting if we have not first addressed their most basic need? Common sense would tell us to meet the basic human need first, and then we can attempt to alter deeper levels of spiritual existence. But it is important to note that there is a way to provide these natural things in a way that would satisfy a hungry heart and quench the thirst of a desperate soul that would lead them toward spiritual fulfillment. We can feed people God's Word but community-focused ministry is about putting our faith in God's word into action. *Faith without works is dead.*[7]

---

[7] James 2:20

If we say we love God and want to serve God, then we must be fully responsible to the gospel. Yes, we say that we are giving them the word, but the question is *how* are we giving them the word? How we break the bread of life makes all the difference to a starving soul. But we must meet them at their point of need. People should feel nurtured when we have provided them a service. A nurturing word of encouragement can help to forever transform someone's life. How we give them the word when they are hungry to hear an inspiring word will make them hungry for more.

In addition, whatever we say should have at least the level of substance that can carry them to the next meal because they truly don't know where this next meal of spiritual nourishment is coming from. And just like they should not feel sick after they eat our natural food, they should not feel ill after they have heard a word from us. We must be careful not to have harassed them instead of embracing them. They should feel emotionally nourished after they eat our spiritual food. There is a distinct difference in the taste of food that has been cooked with love. Similarly, when you prepare a spiritual meal of service, you should do so with love. When we care about the person that we are preparing for we set an atmosphere of caring. Anything less classifies us as goats that are selfish, self-centered, obstinate and rebellious.

"Then shall he say also unto them on the left hand, Depart from me, ye cursed, into everlasting fire, prepared for the devil and his angels":[8]

Jesus is basically telling the people who have the characteristics of goats to "get out of his face." He tells them that they are cursed but it is their own nature and works that have betrayed them. What is also interesting is that they are sent to the lake of fire that was prepared for the devil and his angels…not necessarily for them! That is why the bible says that hell has enlarged itself[9]. But because of their unwillingness to serve others, they have found themselves in this unalterable predicament.

Even though Jesus is expecting us to do four basic things, it was too much for those who are stubborn, pushy, and disobedient.

"For I was an hungred, and ye gave me no meat: I was thirsty, and ye gave me no drink:

"I was a stranger, and ye took me not in: naked, and ye clothed me not: sick, and in prison, and ye visited me not."

What is interesting though is that their fate is sealed and they don't even understand why. Their obstinate

---

[8] Matthew 25:41
[9] Isaiah 5:14

interrogation of the King is indicative of their obnoxious non-discriminate attitude. First of all, a king is to be revered and honored, therefore it is customary to never rebut a king. It is just understood that respect is due a king and sometimes that means that even though you do not agree, you are silent out of your respect. Your silence is also out of the awareness that the King has control over your future. But this obviously is not always the case here. The goats have to have their final say and with their strong-will attitude, they rebut the king with a query of their own.

> *"Then shall they also answer him, saying, Lord, when saw we thee an hungred, or athirst, or a stranger, or naked, or sick, or in prison, and did not minister unto thee?"*

I believe that they truly knew the answer to their question and that they remembered every time that they were neglectful in performing honorable service. But what they did not expect is to be punished for it—and certainly not eternally. It is sad when unrighteous people think that they can get away with hurtful and nasty behaviors just because they think that the conjured, orchestrated service that they are providing is acceptable. These are the same group of people who will say "…Lord, Lord, have we not prophesied in thy name? and in thy name have cast out devils? and in thy name done many wonderful works?" But these people are obviously deluded and full of themselves. Jesus the King sees through this fiasco and his reaction is pretty much the same as for the goats: "And then will I profess unto them, I never knew you: depart from me, ye that work iniquity."[10]

They thought that they could go on forever and arrogantly push their way around and it didn't matter who got hurt. All that mattered is that they got their way into the spotlight. Some people will do anything to get what they want and it doesn't matter whose head they have to butt to get it. Unfortunately, these have run out of time as well as the opportunity to get it right, although I am sure that they had numerous opportunities. It is my prayer that we will never miss another opportunity to rightly minister to Jesus!

Another way that we minister to Jesus besides feeding those in the community both naturally and spiritually is by providing godly hospitality. Jesus said *"you took me in"*.[11] Although it is notable to take anyone into your home, it is equally important that you take them in with a caring heart. This goes back to the idea that every house is not necessarily a home. It is vitally important that we help people with the basic needs but also that we provide their needs holistically with a compassionate attitude. Most people want to be loved and accepted.

---

[10] Matthew 7:23
[11] Matthew 25:35

When we give people shelter, we are providing them with a type of covering and protection. When we are inviting to them, we give them a sense of support that warms the soul and makes a person feel wanted and even needed. When we open up our hearts as well as our homes, we are truly generous indeed. But isn't this what Jesus has done for us? He engrafted us in when we should have been left on the outside of God's Amazing Grace.

Similarly, it is a very simple thing to give people something to wear but I am sure that is not all that Jesus was talking about. The clothing that touches the heart cannot come from the latest designer. When we clothe in love, we intentionally clothe people with prayerful care and concern. We should love them enough to hide a multitude of their sins[12]. Jesus clothes us with his righteousness. If he didn't do that, we would be naked indeed. When we feel covered, we feel secure. We know that our rights are protected and there is no need for alarm.

Finally, Jesus is emphatic about getting us out of our comfort zones. The places he mentions that we should go, many people don't ordinarily frequent. But what Jesus is really talking about here is presence. Sometimes all we have to do is show up and be a presence of his compassion. We don't necessarily have to do anything but be present. This means everything to a lonely forgotten soul. And we don't necessarily have to say anything. Simple

---

[12] 1 Peter 4:8

presence speaks volumes as it relates to empathetic compassion that translated into engaging encouragement.

In other words, there is no convenience of distance here. Yes, it is easy to make a phone call or send a card or an email. But nothing is more powerful than when one is available to sacrificially connect with someone else who may not be able to give anything in return. And it is in this presence that we can offer physical touch that you cannot get from a phone call or a letter. A touch has redeeming qualities and can be quite reconciling. This is why it is important to encourage appropriate embraces in the fellowship of believers because that may be the only human contact that they get all week. This makes it impossible for us to do 10-foot service. This kind of service is up close and personal.

Jesus makes it clear just how valuable this kind of service is. This kind of activity is the raw material that unconditional love is made of. As a matter of fact, it is these random acts of kindness that emphatically gets us on the right side of the throne. The wrong side is reserved for those who believe that this kind of service is not worth the trouble. But I wonder if they had another opportunity to do it all over again, if they would reevaluate the weight of their actions toward "the least of these".

> *"Then shall he answer them, saying, Verily I say unto you, Inasmuch as ye did [it] not to one of the least of these, ye did [it] not to me."*

"And these shall go away into everlasting punishment: but the righteous into life eternal."

We have to wrestle with recognizing the differences with what has eternal value and that which gives a temporary thrill. Rest assured that in the end you will be judged on your service because you will reap what you sow[13]. But more importantly, the totality of our eternity rests upon whether or not we can provide service to people in a loving, caring way that exemplifies the King and His Kingdom. This passage helps us to determine that the culmination of the Kingdom starts right now, right where you are. It doesn't matter what your station or status is in life. It is mandated for everyone from every nation to reach beyond themselves and serve is the foundational requirement to please the King. Here Jesus makes it biblically clear how important it is to do ministry beyond the doors of your church. As a matter of fact, your life depends on it.

---

[13] Galatians 6:7

BEYOND YOUR DOORS MINISTRY ACTIVATION

If today was the White Throne Judgment event, what side would you be on?

What are the activities in your life that can help you make the determination of where you will end up in this story?

How are you fulfilling the Kingdom Mandate every day and in every way?

What can YOU do to help change the trend of community outreach ministry in your area?

Write a personal mission statement as it relates to our biblical mandate. It should only be 1 to 2 sentences and be so compelling that you can remain accountable to it.

CHAPTER 3

Historical Models of Community-Focused Ministry

"And instead of the tithes which the law commanded, the Lord said to divide everything we have with the poor. And he said to love not only our neighbors but also our enemies, and to be givers and sharers not only with the good but also to be liberal givers toward those who take away our possessions." – Irenaeus, 130-200 AD

Throughout the New Testament we see the mandate unfold for community service. Jesus challenges his listeners to determine what the difference is between them and anybody else if they only visit people who visit them.[14] He helps us to see that it is of no real value to the

---

Kingdom of God to only acknowledge those who do the same for us. Here Jesus is challenging us to get out of our comfort zone. He is clearly showing us that if we only wish well those that we love and admire, we are using no real spiritual power. The lesson here is that we should go beyond our normal circle of close friends and extend ourselves to others. But what is also to be noted from the text is that Jesus is using a bit of sarcasm here because even those people whose only concerned is for a favored few are typically narrow minded anyway.

This is made clear because the statements that Jesus uses to teach this message were typically used of those who were being confronting. For example, the context was to those who were just visiting for visiting sake and was not out of heartfelt concern. Or, the phrase he used would be used of those who pay casual respect to a distinguished person, leaving quickly. It could have also been used by persons who casually embraced or even those who kissed a lot to keep one from leaving. Whatever the context, the people got the point. Jesus' message is clear: The "you scratch my back, I'll scratch yours" mentality has no place in the Kingdom of God.

But centuries later, we are dealing with this same issue. This is true even though in the first century, you could tell the difference between the "followers of the Way" and the pagans. There was an obvious difference in the early church followers who were known for providing random acts of kindness to the poor and marginalized.

Their consistent performance of caring deeds proved that they deeply understood the words of Jesus concerning their compassionate interaction with the poor because this work became their worship. This way, whether they realized it or not, they protected and guaranteed their inheritance in the Kingdom of God

In other words, providing community service in the early church was the order of the day for those who called themselves by the name of Christ. This was readily understood as the true mission of the church. Sacrificial giving was a way of life and expected as a moral code in their circles. Although the Christians frequently "held all things in common"[15] in their fellowship, that did not prevent them from sharing their resources with those who were outside of the fellowship. I believe that once they were liberated from the need of personal possessions, releasing all they owned into the fellowship of believers, it was easy to part with their goods in service to others even outside of their fellowship.

To respond to the exhortation from Paul to support widows and orphans[16], they created a support system that addressed the needs of those less fortunate. They cared for the elderly, the widows, and the orphans. They visited the prisoners and caringly attended to those who were sick. There was no mistake that they were living out their

---

[15] Acts 4:32
[16] James 1:21

commitment to the cause of Christ regardless to who was benefiting.

But in our self-centered society, although it is easy to get people to concur that this is important work, it is difficult to get even Christians - especially those living in America - to live out these principles because they are so busy "getting" for themselves, "doing" for themselves and "living" for themselves. But if we are going to be obedient to the scriptures, then we need to be sure that we allow caring for others to find a way into our lives. It is this activity that will actually make the gospel come alive and bring meaning into our lives. Perhaps we can be inspired by the efforts of the early church to make our "walk line up with our talk." Ray Bakke in his book "A Theology As Big As the City" (Bakke 1997), states that:

> *"The Holy Spirit has been gifting the church with leadership continuously and building up Christ's body since the first century."* [17]

And perhaps this is key. We must allow the gifts of the Holy Spirit to empower us to help others within and without our fellowship. In addition, we should acknowledge the leadership gifts that are positioned to equip the church for Christ-centered service. He goes on

---

[17] Bakke, Ray. A theology As Big As The City. InterVarsity Press, Illinois. 1997 p. 190

to cite several ways that the church infiltrated and transformed society:

> *"In about A.D. 140, a letter was written to a government official telling him that Christian were not a threat to the city-rather, they were the conscience or very soul of the city."*[18]

This reminds me of the movie *"Spanglish"*[19] that is about a Mexican woman who works as a housekeeper for a chef and his family, after migrating with her daughter America. She comes to this country for a better life but what she doesn't expected is the relaxed value system that is contaminating her daughter's soul. She becomes the conscience for the family that she works for.

Oftentimes it is acts of kindness that remind us that we have a conscience as well as how to be grateful for the blessings that we frequently enjoy but take for granted. Christians should certainly be accused of being the "soul of the city" and the conscience as well. Here is a list of other valuable community-focused ministry done by the early church that he cites:

---

[18] ibid
[19] *Spanglish* (2004)". Box Office Mojo. http://www.boxofficemojo.com/movies/?id=spanglish.htm. Retrieved August 30, 2009.

"Urban Garbage Collectors (First Century)…garbage collectors they collected and individually buried the bloated, diseased bodies people tossed into the garbage."[20]

Now how's that for an idea for a church business? Garbage collecting then was for those who had died, but today could very well be the way that we grow our dying churches as we find the remains of people's lives who have lost all hope. Here is another way to grow a church:

"An Urban Nursery (Second Century)…church women provided nursing mothers who sat in the public squares, often under pagan statutes, while other women went up and down the streets to collect the unwanted babies abandoned in the night. They brought them, nursed, bathed and raised them."[21]

What a powerful ministry that aligns with the scriptures to train up a child in the way that they "should" go.[22] These women were on a mission as they went on a "baby hunt" to minister into the lives of abandoned children. Bakke then shows us how the early Christians penetrated every place and every space in the entire city

---

[20] Bakke, Ray. A theology As Big As The City. InterVarsity Press, Illinois. 1997 p. 192.
[21] ibid
[22] Proverbs 22:6

and filling them with the presence of God. He writes of Tertullian, the great Church Father and North African lawyer:

"We are but of yesterday, and we have filled every place among you – cities, islands, fortresses, towns, market-places, the very camp, tribes, companies, palace, senate, forum—we have left nothing to you but the temples of your gods." [23]

Would that not be a tribute and a testament to the Church in this day, that we have filled every place? In addition, this would also solve the "building" problem. Instead of churches struggling to find and buy buildings, perhaps we should be better using our resources to serve those less fortunate and fill every "space" with God's presence. Wouldn't that more aptly fulfill the Great Commission[24] than just focusing on getting people in the pews? Those in the early church understood the urgency needed to minister to those who were beyond our doors and were not afraid to get their hands dirty while doing it.

The church today is more equipped than it has ever been to do ministry that extends further than ever before. One excuse that is often used concerns resources. But as

---

[23] Bakke, Ray. A theology As Big As The City. InterVarsity Press, Illinois. 1997 p. 193
[24] Matthew 28:16-20

we can see many of the ways that the early church did community-focused ministry involved little or no resources, just a hearty dose of conviction and compassion. May they ever inspire us.

BEYOND YOUR DOORS MINISTRY ACTIVATION

What speaks to you in this chapter about the historical foundation of community-focused ministry?

Are there any ministries that you could start that resemble those examples of the early church?

How can you use some of these examples to grow your ministry?

What do you think the church must do in order to begin to address its mandate to care for the poor?

PART II

PEERING OUT...
SEEING THE POSSIBILITIES

CHAPTER 4

Contemporary Models of Community-Focused Ministry

I have the privilege of pastoring a church for over 15 years that has embraced community ministry as a way of life for those who call themselves by the name of Christ. But this was not always the case. When I became the pastor, I inherited a large facility but few members. It took everything from those in the congregation to bear the entire burden of the operational expenses of the church. Every church meeting focused around getting more members but not for the benefit of soul winning but for the purpose of meeting expenses. But this is not just our story. It is the story of many struggling churches around the world. You could get so overburdened with the obligations of the overhead of the church that you could easily forget about the disenfranchised.

But one day, all that changed. After being there for just one year, I challenged the church to think about more than just itself. I taught them the scriptures about caring for the needy and helped them to understand that for the church, community ministry is not optional. It did not take long for them to see God's Mandate and how valuable this ministry was to our church.

Although we were able to embrace this understanding, it never ceases to amaze me how many churches just don't get it. In all my years of teaching in the seminary, I was astounded by the very few churches that actually had a community outreach ministry. Most of the focus was on the saints in the church and little attention was given to the "aints" outside of the church. When this happens, the church is little more that a spiritual day care service that focuses on the needs of their spiritually immature.

But this mindset contradicts the scriptures. We are called to minister to those outside of our fellowship. What makes this difficult is that this mission often takes us out of our comfort zone. But we need to figure out how did we get so comfortable in the first place? It is probably due to the fact that we got a slight case of amnesia. We may have forgot how much we were helped by the church to get to where we are today. Most people come to church for the first time because they need help. When they stay to get the help that they need, sometimes they do so well with what the church provides that they do not remember from where they have come. And then there are times where the converse is true. There are those who came to church because it was the "right" thing to do. They feel like they have not done anything particularly wrong and that the church is the best place for them to shine. That is all well and good but it still contradicts the scripture that says we were "...shaped in iniquity, and weaknesses, and we born in sin ..."[25]

When we consider how much we have been helped by Christ through the church then we should maintain a heart of gratitude. This kind of appreciation does something. And most times that "something" is for someone else. I believe this is what Christ was trying to teach us with his own selfless act of the giving of his life for ours. When we look at it this way, what is too valuable for us to give for the cause of Christ? All Jesus wants is asking us to help the "least of these." Jesus said that the poor you will always have with you.[26] And, if we don't help them, who will?

Fortunately for our congregation, we found our niche. And for the past 12 years, our church has provided educational services to our neighborhood's children. With a vision to make a positive impact within the West Philadelphia community, our mission statement was developed and created with the assistance of our staff to read:

---

[25] Psalm 51:5
[26] Mark 14:7

"It is our mission to partner with families in the development of children by providing nurturing care in a morally sound environment. We support education, celebrate cultural diversity and encourage children to achieve their fullest potential by recognizing their gifts, talents and abilities which will ultimately produce positive contributions globally."

Over the years, our community-focused ministry has evolved and been transformed through human and material resources allowing us to be able to provide the following services to our community. We have had the privilege of being funded for our work from local, state, and federal sources. Below is a list of programs that we have provided over the years:

The Cathedral Learning Center (C.L.C.) is licensed by the Department of Public Welfare as a pre-school program serving up to 50 children ages 1-5 years old. CLC emphasizes the promotion of self-esteem and achievement in very young children. CLC is a unique child care center that offers the "I Can Read" curriculum which emphasizes reading at an early age in a literature-rich, nurturing environment that encourages children of all ages to read and write. Books are made available to each child at every level and are encouraged to be avid readers. Research shows the early childhood years from birth to four years old are critical to literacy development.[27]   In addition, it was also found that there is a direct association with reading and the rate of incarceration.[28]   We are intentional to safeguard our children's future by teaching them to read now! In addition, our goal is to have children reading before they leave our preschool program.

The Cathedral Learning Center is dedicated to presenting creative learning experiences and teaching wholesome values in order to help children properly and develop. CLC hires trained and qualified staff that uses every opportunity to teach children good morals along with the complex information necessary to succeed in the world.

CLC transforms into Kiddie Kamp during the summer months where children enjoy more relaxed and creative, vacation-like activities.   CLC children are happily involved in arts and crafts activities, outdoor fun and water play, cookouts, dramatic play, trips and so much more.

The Motivational Achievement Program (M.A.P.) is licensed by the Department of Public Welfare before and after care program providing transportation, homework

---

[27] Kupcha-Szrom, Jaclyn. "Early Language and Literacy Development." Zero To Three. http://www.zerotothree.org/public-policy/policy-toolkit/early-literacywebmarch1-6.pdf.

[28] ProLiteracy America. "U.S. Adult Literacy Programs: Making a Difference." Accessed April 2, 2012.
http://www.proliteracy.org/NetCommunity/Document.Doc?id=18.

assistance and extra-curricular activities for up to 100 Kindergarten – sixth grade students, representing 5 neighborhood schools. Students are escorted and transported to the program. M.A.P. has provided educational enrichment with an arts and cultural theme to community youth since 1998.

Year after year, M.A.P. finds new ways to promote a better quality of life for children with program activities designed to empower local youth by stimulating their creativity while providing the much needed academic support and supervision to students in a caring environment. Another objective of the program is to reduce the alarming rates of violence that takes place when youth are out of school. M.A.P. is academic in nature and creatively uses diverse applications for educational support that recognizes the numerous learning styles of children such as visual, auditory and kinesthetic. This diverse approach helps children to develop and grow and succeed in every area of life.

M.A.P. strives to keep children engaged by offering a multi-disciplinary collection of structured activities that include computers, creative writing, culinary arts, arts and crafts, media arts and math games, as well as workshops in dance, drama, music/voice, drill team, leadership, supervised sports activities, games, snacks and themed presentations. In addition, special attention is paid to children growing developmentally, emotionally, physically and socially by emphasizing cooperative learning, team building games and leadership development opportunities. Self-control and personal discipline skills are developed through sports, games and the arts.

M.A.P actively incorporates high nutritional and physical standards for all of its participants. The Grill Sergeant Healthy Cooking classes are held twice per week. Menus have been designed to further improve overall health which includes preparing healthy meals such as pancakes, real sloppy joes, home-fries and even croissants. Afternoon snacks now include sugar-free jello, rice pudding and fat free dressing and veggies. In addition, M.A.P. does not use sugary drinks for snacks. Safe fresh drinking water is also available to youth at all times. As a result children are excited about eating veggies, even Brussels sprouts... and even like them! Plans are underway to start the Grill Sergeant's Kidz Garden. The Grill Sergeant will take the children from the garden to the table and help them to understand where healthy foods come from!

M.A.P. also engages its students in Health Education Classes twice per week through The Comprehensive Cardiovascular Risk Reduction Project sponsored by The Haddington Community Health Project Collaborative (HCHP), Health Services & Nutrition Subcommittee, West Philadelphia Youth Development Initiative and To Our Children's Future With Health. The program is worked out in 45 minute sessions with a focus on physical activity that is very interactive so that the students are not bored. This physical activity includes jump rope, jogging, fun activities like hop scotch, and line dancing. During the M.A.P. Out-of-School (OST) day, which is approximately 3 hours, students use the computers but not for more than 30 minutes at a time.

M.A.P. transforms into the Techno-Arts Summer Camp (M.A.P.) and includes summer programming with age appropriate activities that include the following offerings:

- Extensive Reading and Math enrichment provided for each child
- Craft, Theater and Mural Arts experiences
- Strategic Thinking Skills enhancement via Brain Games by TASC Staff
- Culinary Classes provided by Grill Sergeant Kitchen Boot Camp
- Skateboarding skills provided by Franklin's Paine
- Bicycle repair and safety skills provided by Bike Works, Inc.
- Martial Arts skills provided by Mr. Kevin Glover and Company
- Swimming and Water Safety awareness provided by the Nile Swim Club & TASC Staff
- Increased Physical Activity provided at PNP Family Play Center

The following skills were reinforced through the "Discover U: Begin With the End in Mind" and "Global U: The Be-Atitudes" curriculums:

Memorization, Reflection, Forecasting, Visual Arts, Team Building, Public Speaking, Creative Writing, Spiritual Sensitivity, Spiritual Awareness, Grooming, Etiquette, Proper Hygiene, Healthy Lifestyle, Meal Planning, Effective Study Habits, Financial Education, Computer Applications, Media Arts, Goal Setting, Research, Journaling, Diversity Appreciation, Multi-Culturalism, Respect, Creative, Introspection, Improvisation, Social Responsibility, etc.

In addition to offering these programs, the Church has been the center for community programs such as the American Association for Retired People (AARP), Town Meeting site for City Council, The Girl Scouts, the Arthur Ashe Tennis Program, Narcotics Anonymous, the Mayor's Literacy and G.E.D. Programs as well as the Adolescent Violence Reduction Partnership.

The Church received a grant from Nonprofit Finance Fund (NFF) to renovate its computer lab followed by a grant from the state to purchase Dell computers. This facility is Internet capable and ready to be utilized as a work ready training facility. In addition, the computer lab is housed in a 10,000 square foot building that is currently underutilized. It is our vision to integrate a job training component to assist families seeking employment.

This is especially important in light of the Pennsylvania Department of Labor and Industry's December 16, 2010 report regarding unemployment rates. According to the department's Center for Workforce Information and Analysis, the leisure and hospitality sector posted a decline of 6,700 jobs, which is its largest single-month decline since March 1993. The city of Philadelphia has, however, implemented a 5 year plan which includes an initiative aimed at improving its efforts surrounding tourism and brand marketing, precipitating a need for a stronger hospitality workforce. Therefore training residents to assume positions in this industry falls directly in-line with the city's 5-year economic development plan.

As you can see, we have come a long way from where we started. And we are not done yet. There are many other things that we desire to do. With the right people and enough resources, anything is possible. There are a multitude of ways that churches can help the marginalized persons in the community; especially those who do not go to our church. Here is a list of areas that a church can provide services to those in their community:

- Physically challenged
- Mentally challenged
- Accessibility
- Chronic diseases
- Parenting classes

- Teen pregnancy
- Cancer survivors
- Lemaze classes/Nursing classes
- Adult day programs
- After school programs
- Child safety registrations
- Voter registrations
- Counseling
- Male health
- Fitness/health clubs
- Job training
- Employment counseling
- Drug rehabilitation
- Alcohol rehabilitation
- Smoking cessation
- Sexual abuse counseling
- Domestic violence crisis center
- Single parents
- Children of prisoners
- Prison visits van rides
- Job re-entry program
- Advocacy
- Juvenile delinquency
- Veterans
- Food, clothing, shelter
- Literacy
- Homelessness

The list could go on and on. As you can see the possibilities are endless. Typically, the area of focus is something that uniquely speaks to the congregation individually and more importantly, what would be a good fit for the people within the ministry. As you go over this list, you will be inspired to think of other ways that you can serve.

Once you make up in your mind that the church is mandated by the gospel to serve the disenfranchised, then you can prepare for an exciting journey of discovery of what it means to obey Christ in this way. In addition, you will be liberated to look beyond yourself to find what you have been looking for all along…meaning. Life gains a sense of meaning when we are doing satisfying work. Then, just like Jesus, we can prove who we are called to serve: others.

There are many churches around the United States that are doing great community work that is related to this list of outreach opportunities. Many are confident that they have targeted a need and set out to fulfill it. They understand the demographics of their neighborhood and use that information to be the most effective. But they have found a way to specifically target a ministry around what they are already doing by setting a goal to fulfill their mission. But they first had a vision to get results.

As you can see there are a variety of services that a church can provide to its community. In the case of developing an accessible ministry, the goal is to make public places more accessible to those who are handicapped and physically challenged. This is one way to show God's Love is inclusive and provides access. Included in this ministry could be advocacy, counseling, referrals as well as a host of other social services that would make the conditions of these persons more livable. This service could also connect them to the specialized resources that they need such as medical equipment and transportation. Most times there are government agencies that provide these services for free but the people who need them are unaware of where to go for help. Training can also be a part of this ministry in areas that could assist the physically challenged individual to become more productive. Creating a support group with community volunteers is also a way to make physically challenged persons feel like they are a part of the larger community. This type of community outreach ministry can also promote the congregation's reputation and help them to be known as a caring congregation and as one that reaches out to those who are often overlooked.

There are other services that a church can provide to its community that focuses on the well-being of the family. Most often parents are struggling with their parenting skills and have little or no support. There aren't enough books in the library to help them understand that rules of parenting are changing in our swiftly shifting world. They need to be trained and affirmed that what they are doing what is in the best interest of their family. This could come in the form of anything from training on discipline to budget counseling. They could also receive referrals for additional support and assistance. You don't have to feel like you have to provide it all. Sometimes the best help is found in a referral. In addition to these, there are countless opportunities to minister to teen unwed mothers with nowhere else to turn. In some cases housing is needed as well as training and employment opportunities.

Affordable after school programs can be organized for the time that children are out of school. What's more, a component of the program could be set up for special needs children. The frustration level of the parent could be lowered by providing testing to children to screen their development for proper placement in school. This little assistance is priceless and can go a long way.

Another area that families need support that is often overlooked is with elderly parents. These parents may have come to the point in their lives where they now need round-the-clock care. This can be frustrating for an adult child who needs to work to support the family and has no long term care benefits from their place of employment. A service that the church can provide to the family can be to direct them to the numerous resources available in the community as well as provide respite volunteers who may be willing to be a companion. Adult day care could be established in the church to meet that need.

In difficult economic times, job readiness programs could be a welcome gesture to any unemployed or underemployed person. The church could offer job counseling and interview preparedness to boost morale before an interview. The community outreach program could contact employers and be a clearinghouse for job opportunities in thc area and even create some of their own. They can also consider being a job training center helping those who need employment counseling service when a career change is involved. A powerful addition to this program would be to create a re-entry program for prisoners who have difficulty getting back into the workforce.

Another area of need in the community is to provide support for persons who are recovering from substance abuse and addictions. With the rising number of code-pendency problems, there has to be a place where people can go to feel safe enough to bare their souls and get to the source of the problems. Furthermore, many addictions mask the source of other problems in the person's life which can be managed with compassionate professional support.

If the church has property it could take on the challenge to provide affordable housing to elderly or low-income families in the community. Although the responsibilities involved in this undertaking are great, the results can be remarkable in what it means to the families served. A word of caution is warranted here. As well meaning as a church desires to be, sometimes we make tremendous efforts to help people in the difficult seasons in their life and they don't always appreciate the assistance that we are providing nor do they understand the tremendous sacrifice that is being made to make their lives easier. But what really matters here is the mandate that Jesus has given. He is pleased with our commitment to feed the hungry, clothe naked, visit the sick and offer hospitality with compassion regardless of how it is perceived in our time and throughout eternity.

The opportunities are as endless and as diverse as the make-up of the strength, talents and abilities of the members of the congregation to the distinct nature of the community itself. Each congregation should find its niche…and scratch it!

BEYOND YOUR DOORS MINISTRY ACTIVATION

What are the talents, abilities and giftings of the members of your congregation that would facilitate a unique community-focused ministry? List them here:

Do a S.W.O.T. of your congregation. (Strengths, Weakness, Opportunities, and Threats) See the Index for this matrix.

Given your resources, what would you determine as the most viable ministry that your church could provide? List them here:

CHAPTER 5

Seven Vital Steps to Start a Community-Focused Ministry

C hurches should already exist to contribute to the community by cultivating the biblical values therein. The overall objective here is to help churches to become successful at providing community-focused ministry that focuses on improving the quality of lives of persons within the community where there is a church presence. It has been found that a community fares better by virtue of the fact that there is a church in the neighborhood. But only about 15% of the immediate community will be directly impacted by the church's presence with church attendance or church participation. 85% of the people are relatively lost. The question that remains is what will we do about the 85%?

Research done by the Barna Group[29] regarding church life and spirituality relating to church effectiveness revealed that churches are making a difference in their communities in a variety of ways. But it was also found that the most effective ministry for a church to do in a post Christian society is work that advances and improves the quality of life in children and youth. It was discovered that this type of work promises to be the most effective, with far reaching, long lasting benefits in helping persons to achieve their fullest potential. Areas that specifically affect the quality of life of children fall into three basic categories: education, housing, food and clothing.

- Food/clothing has been a traditional emphasis of churches and fits the mandate by God to feed the hungry and clothe the naked. This is good work but there is uncertainty of the rate return on investment as it relates to the long term material and spiritual development of persons. People who come only for these items may never return for a church service or for further ministry and help in other areas. They are merely concerned with the need for the moment and therefore there is very little opportunity to create social change. There

---

[29] Dr. George Barna, Leadership Secrets for Cutting Edge Distinction" (lecture, May 31, 2010, Milwaukee, WI).

are some ministries who have identified this problem and won't give out any items until the persons listen to a gospel message. Whether or not this is effective is equally uncertain. The church must discover new and creative ways to "give" in a way that evokes transformation.

- Housing development is also important but a bit more difficult because of the work involved on many different levels that include municipalities, zoning, businesses, and other organizations whose specialty it is to govern sizable housing projects. This is possible but only those with the capacity to "count the cost" should attempt such feats.

- Educational ministry to children and youth appears to have the most potential for positive outcomes, the greatest return on investment, and can be workable for almost any size ministry. In addition, this work can take shape in a variety of ways.

Whichever area of focus for community ministry that the church seeks to provide is contingent upon the context and the direct needs of the neighborhood residents. It is vitally important that church leaders get the facts, information, and training necessary to implement a community-focused ministry in their neighborhood that adequately addresses these areas. This valuable information will help the servant leader to make informed decisions and think critically about how to effectively strategize to better serve its community. What follows are the critical steps for a servant leader to take in developing a community-focused ministry:

1. <u>Establish a sense of call</u> - What must first be established is an understanding about where you are as a leader and your perception concerning community-focused ministry. Get a sense of what is your specific call to do this kind of work. This call should be based upon a biblical principal. As you study God's Word around the subject, it will provide the foundational support that you need to launch a work and also serve as a reminder of your call even in difficult times. This call could also focus on a personal issue or experience that speaks directly to you. Most times it is what is personal that we are most passionate about.

   Then, the leader needs to determine what their role will be in that ministry. Sometimes leaders and pastors desire to see community-focused ministry fulfilled in their churches but they are unwilling to get their hands dirty with the business of connecting with people other than their members. But in order for community-focused ministry to be the part of the culture of your church, you must be willing to make an investment of yourself, your resources, and your energies. This is especially true in order to get it off the ground.

It is important that the leader model the passion for community-focused before the congregation or they will assume that this mandate is an optional idea easily left to someone else. The servant leader must thoroughly embrace this model of ministry as the mandate of the Kingdom of God as outlined in Matthew 25:31-46 and be willing to help others to do the same. The leader must personally embody the vision and the mission before the people will ever support it. The servant leader must have developed a personal theology for community ministry. They must ground this theology with a biblical foundation on which they can move forward to determine the ways that the Church can fulfill its Kingdom Mandate.

In some cases, this will be difficult because many people in church do not get the reality that the church exists for more than just its members. So the servant leader has to help the congregation become more intentional about getting out of its self-centered comfort zone. If the church is not already doing some type of community-focused ministry, the servant leader needs to explore the reasons why not and determine how the church got away from its original mission. This could be unsettling as the query may uncover personal obstacles and even pose a threat to the well-being of the congregation. This is because when you inquire about what prevents your church from fulfilling its mission to the community then you are going to also ask an even more important question: Who is keeping us from fulfilling our mandate to serve our community? The answers may be startling because in some cases that person is the leader.

The answer for what the church is called to do in reaching out to the community should be found in the leader's prayer life. It is in prayer that the leader should hear God's voice and particular mandate for the house of worship that they have been assigned. We should never underestimate the power of prayer although it is highly underrated. It is in this time that the leader should also make the biblical connection concerning the community outreach ministry as a foundation upon which to build. Once it is clear in the mind of the leader that it is imperative that your congregation is engaged in community-focused ministry, then you have to determine what your role will be in helping to change the trend of community outreach ministry in the church.

I have found that pastors who do not have a passion for community-focused ministry have a difficult time actually sustaining the same. Therefore it is critical that the pastor creates his/her own personal mission statement that is compelling enough to hold the leader accountable to their own vision to provide community-focused service. This statement should be unique to the person in their particular context. It can also be based upon the scripture reference that will be used as the foundation upon which you build your outreach ministry. What is critical here is that you are able to articulate what you feel driven to do. This is important because you need to communicate this with others who you need to help you to accomplish your goal. Secondly, when things do not turn out or look the way that you think they should, you can always refer back to your own personal mission to support the vision that you have in your heart. For every vision, God does have a provision. This personal mission statement will also give you a sense of conviction. Having a sense of conviction will create a sphere of responsibility that regardless of what it looks like you know what you "must" do.

2. <u>Get to know your community</u>. - The best way to intelligently understand what your community needs is by research through demographics. Do your homework and concentrate your research on your zip code or no more than a half mile radius. Demographics will inform you with the facts about the age, race, ethnicity, income, education, gender, religion, etc. regarding the people in your community. You do not have to guess at what your neighborhood is like based on the few people that you see when you are there. You can know with certainty these things about your community by looking at the facts con-

tained in the demographics. This is especially important before you prepare to minister to the community. This will also prevent you from making a lot of assumptions as well as a lot of mistakes. One place that you can go is to <u>www.FreeDemographics.com</u> for more info.

Another way to get to know your community is to take a walk around to see what is going on there at different times of the day. Do a pray walk around your community and pray for the neighborhood as the needs that you see arise. This should also be done on a regular basis each and every time you drive around the neighborhood as you come and go. Pray that God would speak to you with clarity regarding the needs of the people and those in particular that God has specifically called you to meet. In addition, this is a great time to take spiritual authority in your community by decreeing and speaking life into the neighborhood. Declare the things that you believe that God wants to see there. Commit to participate with God as well as with other community members to fulfill God's Vision for your community.

3. <u>Research your specific neighborhood</u>. Determine the assets and the liabilities that are already there. This is a good time to also determine who else is doing your brand of community service. You should make every effort to build relationships with these organizations. These people should become your partners or at least

your resource for information on best practices. The bible informs us that *"There is nothing new under the sun."[30]*You do not have to reinvent the wheel. Create a network so that you have a built in support system. Expose the people to the ministry that you want to see. Research what issues need to be addressed with other organizations so that you can learn from their experiences and be ahead of the game. Another form of research includes customized surveys. It is important that you get the opinion of the people that you would like to service and target their needs. Customize your survey to get the answers that you need. Ask the right questions to get the right answers. For example, stay away from closed ended questions like: Do you need help? The only answer would be "Yes" or "No." Ask questions like which of the following ways can we assist you? And then list the ways that you feel certain that you can provide assistance. Also leave a space for them to comment so that they can provide you with some much needed information that you may have not anticipated.

Position yourself to do effective service with the facts from the clientele that you intend to serve. You do not have to use your imagination when it comes to community-focused ministry. The last thing that we should do is assume we know how to help a per-

---

[30] Ecclesiastes 1:9

son in need. We should simply ask them. When we do this, we can provide effective service in filling a real, felt need. Effective service is service that hits the mark leaving people feeling cared for. And isn't that what Jesus expects from us? When appropriately asked, people will readily tell you exactly what they need. The question is "are you prepared to meet that need?"

4. <u>Organize</u> – Organization is the key to your success. The five "W"'s will help you to respond appropriately.

a) <u>Who</u>? – The first "who" will involve those who will supporting the community-focused service that you intend to provide? Choose people from your ministry and community that can make it happen. Stack the deck with staff that has a passion for the particular service that you want to provide. These people should also comprise your planning team. They will help you create a framework by which the ministry is developed that includes your mission statement, goals, and guidelines. They should also help you to do the research needed to identify the current needs as well as the available resources in your community.

These people could also serve as your board of directors when and if you decide to create a community development corporation. This depends upon the amount and length of commitment they are willing to give. It is important to establish what this commitment is so that you can understand an appropriate timeline for the planning stages of your community-focused ministry. Some may only feel called to help you plan. Others may have the desire to serve as an officer and even a staff person once the planning stage is over. Whatever roles each person takes on, this should be supported by a job description so that everyone is clear about what to do and what needs to be done. This also avoids confusion because everyone is clear about what each person on the team is doing and helps everyone to stay in their lane. We will talk more about board involvement later in the chapter on the ABC's of CDCs (Community Development Corporation).

As a general rule, you should never do community-focused ministry alone. Not only does this defeat the purpose of a community-focused ministry but it also does not afford you the support that you need to pull it off successfully. You will need to gather information, plan, execute, and provide adequate service. If you cannot find anyone to support your vision to do community ministry then it is not time to do it. Pray and wait until God sends someone who can co-labor with you on your dreams. This is also important because in the event of an emergency, you will need someone who can take over for you if something suddenly happens to you. This is why many community outreach ministries fail because they cannot be consistently maintained by only one person. Build a fail-proof ministry so that your "fruit will remain."[31]

The next and most important thing that you have to determine is "who" is the face of the demographic that you want to serve? Is it teen mothers?…or young men prone to gang violence? Your demographic study will help you hone in on "whom" in your community needs you the most. The face you choose should also be the person who you have the capacity for and are able to successfully serve.

Another important "who" includes other community leaders and representatives that you should connect with that will make your job easier. It is vital to build relationships with your council persons, congresspersons and state representatives, and even the mayor of your city. These political people have the connections that you need to make inroads into your community and you need to make sure that they know you personally. Furthermore, you should let these people know that you are a stakeholder in the communi-

---

[31] John 15:16

ty and that you are committed to making a difference. Make them aware of your agenda and the way in which you want to serve your community. Be a part of their team and let them know that you will support them as well so that you are all on the same page. The saying, "it's not what you know but 'who' you know", works tremendously well when doing community-focused ministry. Take advantage of it and you will find that it will become easier to reach your goal. It is also critical for you to get to know your local neighborhood business owners and bank managers. These partnerships will prove important when you are ready to take action.

b) <u>What</u>? - So now that you know to whom you will provide a service, what exactly is the service that you want to provide? What will you do with these persons? Will you teach them? Counsel them? Train them? Mentor them? What exactly will you do? You can answer these questions by determining the ultimate outcomes that you want to see. What are your short and long term goals? Knowing these items can better inform you as you create your mission statement. Please refer to the "Plan of Action" (P.O.A.) Chart in the Index to help you to answer these questions. This P.O.A is based upon the Logic Outcomes Model[32]

In addition, it is important to set out to only do what you have the capacity to do. Anything else will not be to your advantage. Each church has a signature outreach that they can do well. You must determine how far that reach extends. If all of the churches in the community did well what they could do, then most of the unmet needs in the community would be satisfied. One church will never be able to meet all of the needs but you can determine what you can effectively address and do that, well. You can establish which assignment in the community that will be by doing a thorough assessment of what that is.

Another "what" involves what you will say about your community outreach ministry. What will it be called? What catchy slogans will you use to make your outreach appealing to those who serve as well as those you want serve? A note of warning: the people who have not ever been to church may not understand what a "St. Stephen's Outreach" ministry is but they will have some idea about what you are trying to accomplish if

---

[32] Weiss, C.H. (1972), Evaluation Research. Methods for Assessing Program Effectiveness. Prentice-Hall, Inc., Englewood Cliffs, New Jersey

you called it the "Motivational Achievement After-School Program." Furthermore, it is best to
give thoughtful consideration to the names of
ministries. If you are ministering to former drug
dealers or prostitutes, it may not be a good idea
to call it the "Drug Dealer and Prostitute Ministry." I know that this sounds far-fetched but it is
as risky as calling a ministry that helps people
with drug and alcohol problems the "Drug and
Alcohol Ministry." Is that the outcome that you
want to see? This ministry should be designed to
produce positive outcomes and should be called
as such. How about a name like "Forever Free"?

While I am on this subject, all funders do not
go to church. That means that you have to be
careful not to use a lot of church jargon when
communicating with them. "What" you say is
just as important as how you say it. It is not appropriate to greet a congressperson the way you
would greet one of your church members. And it
is definitely not advised to use this as an opportunity to witness to them. Your desire to support
your community is witness enough. Should the
occasion arise and they ask you to pray for a
loved one and they seek your assistance, take the
marvelous opportunity, but please be sensitive
enough not to abuse the privilege. Use tact and
discretion.

A final "what" relates to the polity of your church. What is the policy for starting a ministry in your church...in your community? What are the steps that you need to take in order to get the ball rolling within the structure of your ministry? Outline those steps and follow through with your plan. Don't stop until you complete it. Do not move forward until you accomplish your goal of determining the best way to establish a community-focused ministry in your church that is mutually beneficial to your church and community. This is also indicative of the level of outreach ministry that you are able to provide. You may only be able to reach the people on your block. Or you may feel that you can tackle your entire community's needs in a particular area of ministry whether it is to help the elderly, youth, housing, food, etc. After you determine what level or quality of ministry that you can provide, you may also want to determine what other resources on the local, state and national levels are available to assist you in your endeavors.

This is also the area that you determine what resources you are able to dedicate to the community outreach ministry. When considering this, you must put together a budget of items that you need for the project. Even if things are expected to be donated, they still have an in-kind value.

You will need these values later when you want to put together a proposal for a funder. In addition, you want to be prepared to financially support the ministry in the event that those well meaning persons who gave can no longer support you. Remember everything cost something! Put it on the budget.

c) <u>When</u>? – A real important question to answer is when will you provide the service? At what time of the day, month or year will it be feasible for you provide this service? You will have a good idea about this if you have appropriately polled the constituency that you are looking to serve. This information will help with the scheduling of other ministry work as well as gauge what is convenient to the population that you want to serve.

d) <u>Where</u>? – At what location will this service be provided? Don't assume that it will be at the church. Some churches have the space for it and others do not. But this should not prohibit the work. Depending upon the area of service, the church may not be the best location. It could be a nearby coffee house that allows the participants feel more comfortable or it may be at the local gym. You can be as creative as your imagination will allow. But whatever you do make sure that your location is clean and accessible and consistently available. In addition, you will need to factor in if there is a cost to any location that is chosen and be sure to put that on the budget.

e) <u>Why</u>? – This is probably the most important question of all because answering this question will determine the answer to the "How?" question. When you understand why you are doing something and you have a conviction about it, this determines how and how well you will do it. When thinking about why you are doing your type of community service, "begin with the end in mind"[33] What are the outcomes that you want to see? Remind yourself that you are working hard because you want to see a particular behavior change or you desire that people are more aware on a particular issue. By doing this you are clear about why you set out to do your service in the first place.

5. <u>Create the atmosphere</u> – This is going to take preparation. Preparation is the key if you want your church or organization to buy into your vision. A pastor can prepare the congregation for community-focused ministry endeavors by preaching on the subject. The Good Samaritan story is a great place to

---

[33] Covey, Stephen R. *The 7 Habits of Highly Effective People*. New York: Free Press, 2004.

start. Teachers can tie information about what is going on in the community into their lessons. All other leaders can help with the communication process to members by sharing their voice and lending their prayerful support. You can also rally volunteers and donations with specific worship services that focus on blessing the people who are to be served in the community ministry. Get them involved and let them tell their story. When people hear it first hand, they are more inclined to embrace the community effort. Brochures, flyers, banners, letters, etc. will be vital in creating an environment of caring that is sympathetic to your cause. Before you do it, let them see it. Without a vision the people perish[34]

6. <u>"Just do it!"</u>[35] Be sure to set a launch date and then proceed as scheduled. Create a timeline so that you can build momentum as you approach the release date. Continue to plan and envision along the way. See it through from start to finish. Set targets, benchmarks, and milestones. Assure in writing what you want to see happen by a certain time and stay on track. Set your objectives and accomplish your goal. Ask "What are we going to do about the problem in

---

[34] Proverbs 29:18

[35] Center for Applied Research. "Nike's "Just Do It" Advertising Campaign." http://www.cfar.com/Documents/nikecmp.pdf.

our community?" ... and then set out to solve the problem. Replace the undesirable condition with the desired outcomes. But don't just keep planning. When you are done with your planning, move into action and mobilize.

7. <u>Evaluate</u> – It is very important to incorporate evaluation into the process of creating a community-focused ministry. Also address the fact that it you may not have done everything right and that it is okay to fail. This is important especially if this is your first time. If what you set out to do did not work, stop and change where necessary but do not get discouraged. Use your previous experience as a springboard to get you to the next level. Use whatever did not work as a learning and start the process all over again, but this time smarter and wiser. When you are completed planning your community-focused ministry, consider utilizing these S.M.A.R.T. goals as an assessment:

<u>Specific</u> - Make sure that what you want to do is clear and concise. "Write the vision, make it plain."[36] Too often we don't accomplish our goals because they are either too broad or too general, or too overbearing.

<u>Measurable</u> – There are some things that we want to do and this is great but we won't know when we have

---

[36] Habakkuk 2:2

met our objectives because we cannot measure the results. Measurable results are those that can be quantified. For example: You can set a goal to help 10 young girls learn more about entrepreneurship. You know that they understand it by giving them a pre- and a post-test. This way you can specifically measure how much they have learned after your service.

Attainable - Set specific manageable goals that are relatively easy to accomplish. Be careful not to set goals too large. Allow yourself the opportunity to build up your confidence and accomplish small goals, then you can set out to do more. Start small and work your way up.

Realistic – It is not just the size of the goal that can be unrealistic. Sometimes it is the timeframe by which you want to accomplish it. You may set a goal for a women's group to join your community health club and lose 100 pounds in 30 days but is that realistic? Or you may expect that 50 people will be present on the first day of your English as a Second Language class but you only invited five. Is that realistic? Setting a manageable and realistic goal is easier in a pilot program. When you start your community program in a pilot program, you give yourself the opportunity to put the work under a microscope and test the results against researched data. This takes the edge off determining whether you succeeded or failed. What is important is that you did something and moved forward.

<u>Time-Based</u> – Timing is everything! Set an expectation for the timeframe that you want to realize your future outcomes. Don't stop until you see the fruit of your labors. Set reasonable timelines for expected results. Plan the work and consistently work the plan. If you set a specific time that you want to complete your project then you will know if you accomplished the goal or not by merely looking at the calendar or if you need to set more time.

Here I have outlined some ways to begin a community-focused ministry so what are you waiting for?

BEYOND YOUR DOORS MINISTRY ACTIVATION

In Matthew 28:19, In his last words to His disciples, Jesus commands us to go and teach all nations...What are some things that you can teach?

As you commit to teach are you also willing to commit to learn?

What are you willing to do to prepare yourself to provide informed community ministry?

What is your Plan of Action (P.O.A.) See Index Fig 1.

CHAPTER 6

Community-Focused Ministry Draft

O nce you have done your homework and started your community-focused ministry service and are experiencing some kind of success, you may start to think about taking your community outreach ministry "to the streets." This may mean seeking outside funding for your project to provide resources to help you to expand your work to a greater number of participants or provide a broader range of services. Perhaps you want to expand to cover a greater area or even hire more staff. There are times when you want to do more but you are limited by your resources. There are various grants and funding opportunities available to the general public through private and government funding.

Most often these grants are very competitive and are reserved for the experienced grant writer for which you may or may not want to hire. On the other hand you may find the particular funding opportunity that you have the capacity to take advantage of. The first thing that you need to do is create what is called a boilerplate for your organization. The boilerplate is an industry term that originated with the steel industry in the 1800's and was the information that was affixed to the boiler so that people would know who the manufacturer was. It was the same information pressed out over and over. When you apply this to your organization, it is the standardized information that you add to all of your documents so that people can know something about your organization.

This boilerplate should be approximately one paragraph and include all of the facts about your organization. Be sure that your unique boilerplate includes the following:

- Name of ministry or CDC;
- Location and web address;
- Years in existence;
- Ministry focus/size/effectiveness;
- Community focus;
- Your asset to your community; or
- What is your unique footprint in your community?
- If you already have a community-focused ministry, how will you expand, improve for the future? This is called a positioning statement that says something convincing about what you do well that makes you stand out from the rest.

By this time you probably realize that you have to contextualize your language. Although you may be a church leader, you must be careful about the language that you use when talking to funders. Servant leaders must be willing to learn how to speak more than one language especially if they are planning to receive funding from private and governmental institution. The reason is because of the legality of the separation of Church and State. The government wants to make sure that their money is not being used for evangelistic purposes. Even though that is one mission of the church, it is not the mission of the government. Furthermore, it is critically important that you understand the fact that once you receive a grant, you are obligated to serve everyone in the community. This is important because you are required to service people regardless of race, religion or creed so be prepared for this.

Funders regularly put out Requests for Proposals (RFPs) or Request for Applications (RFAs) which are self explanatory. Please give the fund only the information that they asked for. Adding additional information may not be to your advantage. Most grant proposals are ranked based upon how well the submitter was able to follow instructions and give the information requested within the confines of the request. One of the biggest mistakes that one can make is not to follow the instructions to the letter. If the funder is asking you to state in 500 words or less why you think that you should receive the money, then don't submit 1,000 thinking that you are being impressive. Sometimes less is more and it is more important that you say what you need to with the least amount of words with an emphasis upon clarity. You should be as concise as possible and don't waste your words. Rather, tell the funder exactly what they want to hear in your own words. Assure them that you understand what their expectations are and are willing to meet the guidelines, quotas and all expectations with excellence. Don't be afraid to "toot your own horn." Funders need to know about the great work that you do in order to make a final decision. Readers who judge the grant may be swayed with one grant over the other just because you took the time to share your great track record in the appropriate place on the application.

Pay attention to deadlines. Due to the competitive nature of grants, funders set and keep deadlines. Get in the habit of not waiting until the last minute to finish a grant. You can't imagine how many times I have finished grants way ahead of schedule only to find out that I was missing a document. I had just enough time to find it or request it from another agency. Leave enough time to get what you need to present. Additionally, you must pay attention to the deadline in other time zones.

If you have a solid draft of your community outreach ministry already done, all you have to do is cut and paste bits and pieces of information into the application rather than starting from scratch. This saves valuable time especially when you are in a time crunch. The following should be a well thought out plan for your ministry in draft form ready for any opportunity for any grant-making occasion that arises. It should include an outline of a practical community ministry opportunity or possibility at your current ministry setting with the following and should include the following components:

- Community demographics demarking boundaries of which the information is from including the zip code information and or territorial community boundaries;
- The specific needs that will be addressed including the results from a survey of persons to be impacted by the community-focused ministry;
- Research of similar programs and list of contacts of resources and referrals;
- The process of implementation within a particular church polity, or community organization.

Also to be included are program specifics such as:

- The budget;
- Any special needs;
- Staffing requirements;
- Any legal requirements;
- Current funding sources;
- Space requirements.

A final reflection of the potential, projected success and evaluation of the ministry program is needed to pitch and position the community-focused ministry to the right people. This is important especially if you desire to get funding from outside sources. If this is the case be prepared to participate in areas of :

- Collaborative planning;
- Community action;
- Community change;
- Capacity building;
- Producing deliverables and outcomes;
- Adapting to a professional environment;
- Building competency;
- Community institutionalization.

Be prepared to discuss the challenges as well as the opportunities. Be sure to outline all activities that will be accomplished by the collaborative leadership to support the community organizations. Create the model to facilitate the process of community empowerment.

When considering any partnerships, it is best to explore a synergistic/team based model. This model provides the organization with the human resource that it needs in order to thrive and depends upon the rich acumen of individual strengths. This model operates from the premise that everyone brings something to the table. The organization functions more intelligently because information and knowledge is shared readily and completely. The success of this leadership model depends upon a balanced combination of expertise. This also aids in the expediting of the process involved in decision making. Additionally, this presents a better platform for the leveraging of resources.

When resources are pooled there is a greater likelihood of success and commitment to the team because there is a common purpose. It is critical to keep open lines of communication in order to establish and achieve the goal.

Archimedes said about 2,500 years ago: "Give me a place to stand and I can move the earth." Archimedes was talking about leverage! The bible says "How can two walk together except they be agreed?"[37] With a collaboration and range of resources, you can agree together to move anything!

---

[37] Amos 3:3

BEYOND YOUR DOORS MINISTRY ACTIVATION

What are some ways that you can learn the language of your potential funder?

Do a Google search on the Internet relating to your ministry interest. What have you discovered?

What are the political assets that could help you to establish your community-focused ministry?

PART III

TAKING IT TO THE STREETS

CHAPTER 7

The ABC's of CDC's

A Community Development Corporation (CDC) is a broad term that refers to non-profit organizations that incorporate for the purpose of improving the quality of life of a community in some way. This may include programs and services providing activities that promote and support the well-being of the community. This is unique from a for profit organization whose ultimate agenda is to make a profit. This for profit agenda may not be in the best interest of the community. CDCs typically serve a specific geographic location such as a neighborhood or a town. They often focus on serving lower-income residents or struggling neighborhoods. CDCs can be involved in a host of activities that include economic development, education and empowerment through real estate development or entrepreneurship.

CDCs can be formed by residents, small business owners, congregations and other local stakeholders to revitalize their low and/or moderate income community. CDCs typically produce affordable housing and create jobs for community residents. Some CDCs also provide a variety of social services to their target area.

CDCs can maintain a diverse focus such as real estate development that creates affordable housing, or economic development that gives small business lending, technical assistance and small business incubation that provides space at a nominal fee or no cost at all. CDCs can focus on education and training through early childhood education, workforce training, non-profit incubation as well as youth and leadership development, and advocacy.

A Community Development Corporation is considered a nonprofit corporation with a group of people who join together to do some activity that benefits the public, such as running community health programs or domestic violence shelters. It is a corporation formed to carry out a charitable, educational, religious, literary or scientific purpose. A nonprofit corporation doesn't pay federal or state income taxes on profits it makes from activities in which it engages to carry out its objectives. This is because the Internal Revenue Service (IRS) and state tax agencies believe that the benefits the public derives from these organizations' activities entitle them to a special tax-exempt status.

There are a variety of groups, from artists and musicians to people active in education, health and community services who wish to operate as nonprofit (or not-for-profit) corporations. Often the reason for doing this is simple -- nonprofit status is usually a requirement for obtaining funds from government agencies and private foundations.

CDCs can be created to have a direct impact on community planning and community organization or form to have a direct influence over them. A Community Development Corporation is a general term that is often used by different types of non-profit associations. A Community Development Corporation could be organized to address an existing problem within a certain neighborhood or be formed to support another group that does the same.

The corporation is modeled after the standard business model and can be considered a business opportunity whose objective is to provide services to support the community directly related to a current need or problem within a specific area. Most times CDCs use OPM (Other People's Money)! A CDC is legally the same as any other non-profit entity organized under section 501 (c) (3) of the Internal Revenue Code. Organizations that are interested in forming a CDC should:

Choose a legal business name before you decide to form your nonprofit community development corporation. You should follow the guidelines and comply with the rules of your state's corporate filing office and make sure that the business name meets the requirements of state law. This could be considered the same as creating a fictitious name. Before making an application you should make sure that the unique name you choose is available.

Assure that the name you choose for your nonprofit is not the same as the name of another corporation on file. It is important to call ahead before filing the application. In addition to confirming that another nonprofit corporation isn't already using your proposed name in your state, make sure that your organization's name will not violate any trademarks owned and registered by another company in the country. Conduct a trademark search. For information about trademark law and name conflicts go to http://www.uspto.gov for more information.

Please note that half of the states in America require that the name you choose ends with a corporate designator. This would include suffixes such as Corporation, Incorporated, Limited, or Corp., Inc., or Ltd. You must be certain that the name you select does not contain certain words prohibited by the state, such as Cooperative, Federal, National, United States, Bank, or Reserve.

Once you've selected an available and legal name, you may have to file to reserve the name in your state. This may also be done when you file your articles of incorporation. In some cases, when you file your nonprofit's articles of incorporation, your name will be automatically registered. Please check the regulations as the rules differ depending upon the state. To file formal paperwork, usually called articles of incorporation, you will also have to pay a small filing fee (approximately under $100).

After you've decided on your business name, remember that you must prepare and file articles of incorporation[38] with your state's corporate filing office. You must file "articles of incorporation" with your jurisdiction's Secretary of State's Corporations Division.

This document may also need to be submitted with the filing of the application for your organization's name. This document may be called a different name in your state and instead may use the term articles of organization, certificate of incorporation, certificate of formation, or charter. Please see IRS Publication 557 - Sample of Articles of Organization (p.69) for more information.

Once you file for incorporation with your state incorporation office next you must apply to the federal IRS for designation as a tax exempt, non-profit organization under the 501 (c) 3 IRS code. This is the most common federal tax exemption status, which is why nonprofits are frequently referred to as 501(c)(3) corporations. This IRS designation is necessary in order for organizations to be recognized a charitable organization that can obtain

---

[38] http://www.irs.gov/pub/irs-pdf/p557.pdf, Section 501(c)3 articles of an organizations (p.26)

grants and gifts from the government. In addition, corporate, foundations and private sources are eligible for a tax deductible receipt for their donations.

Obtaining grants; is only one reason to incorporate. There are two other important reasons why forming a nonprofit organization is done. One is to have the benefit of tax-exempt status to keep from having to pay taxes and other is protection from personal liability.

If your organization becomes the target of a lawsuit, incorporation can provide security to its members. What is also important to note is the protection from personal liability for the group's activities. Although nonprofit corporations can and will be sued, The protection from personal liability is afforded to the members and the directors where the incorporation exists. This simply means that their personal possession, money, houses, cars or other property aren't at risk in the event of a lawsuit.

It is also important to keep in mind that if the organization does advocacy activity, it could provoke legal battles. There are rulings and tax exempt status for nonprofits to be able to engage in political advocacy. Those advocacy efforts could engage a nonprofit into an unwanted lawsuit. By choosing to appropriately engage in lobbying under special regulation, the incorporation efforts can protect the members, and officers in the event of a lawsuit but this should be determined well in advance.

There are various stages that an organization can go through during start up of a nonprofit venture and there are various stages that the organization can development. Forming a nonprofit corporation is very similar to forming a regular corporation.

It may be in the best interest though to intentionally take the stages in steps rather than complete all of the stages at once. Some organizations start out informally, organized around a particular mission and continue to grow with their programs and activities. As long as their revenues do not exceed $25,000 per year and the organization does not employ anyone, there is no need to file anything further.

But as the organization's interest, activities and donations grow, the organization may need to become more fiscally responsible with reporting requirements as well as administrative tasks. This may be a great opportunity to extend their tax-exempt status to a for-profit organization with valuable tax credits if they agree to help them in their efforts to help the community. This partnership allows the community development organization to continue to focus on the mission of the programs and allow the for profit professionals to handle the arduous task of handling the business. This way, the organization can then simply incorporate at the state level and maintain fiscal accountability. Finally, the organization can apply for its 501(c)3 tax-exempt status from the Internal Revenue Service.

Once accepted, the organization can accept tax-deductible donations and is responsible for following regulations set by the IRS and the state, and for reporting annually to the IRS, Secretary of State's Office, and Attorney General's Office. If the organization makes a profit from its programs and activities, becoming a nonprofit corporation can yield a great benefit. This is because as long as the money you make is related to your charitable work, your nonprofit corporation won't be required to pay income tax on it.

It is required that you submit a copy of your filed articles with your application to IRS. After the corporate filing office in your state returns a copy of your filed articles, you can then submit your federal 501(c)(3) tax exemption application to the IRS and include them with your application. Use Form 1023 Application for Recognition of Exemption Under Section 501(c)(3) of the Internal Revenue Code. There is currently a Filing fee of $850. This is a critical step in the formation of your nonprofit organization since most of the real benefits of being a nonprofit flow from 501(c)(3) tax-exempt status.

But, simply filing nonprofit incorporation forms do not automatically make the organization tax exempt. You must also complete federal and state application forms for tax exemptions. If necessary, you can apply for state tax exemption. In a few states (California, Montana, North Carolina, and Pennsylvania), you must complete a separate application to get a state tax exemption. In other states, as long as you file nonprofit articles of incorporation and obtain your federal 501(c)(3) tax-exempt status, your state tax exemption will be automatically granted. In still others, to get your state exemption you must send in a copy of the IRS determination letter that granted your federal exemption. Contact your state tax agency to find out what steps you must take.

If your organization wants to apply for public or even private grant money, it is unlikely you qualify without tax-exempt status. Some groups try to form a nonprofit, tax-exempt association, rather than a corporation. But this makes it more difficult to qualify for a tax exemption. Forming a tax exempt association requires the preparation and adoption of complicated organizational papers and cumbersome operating rules. Therefore it is generally easier to get the IRS to approve a tax exemption for a nonprofit corporation. If your organization becomes a tax-exempt nonprofit corporation, and wants to solicit tax-deductible contributions, donors can deduct their gifts to your group on their federal and state income tax returns.

It is important to note here that churches automatically have tax-exempt status. Their donors can legally deduct their contributions on the federal and state income tax returns.

There are additional benefits of organizing a non-profit corporation. Nonprofits can apply for and receive a mailing permit that gives them a special reduced non-profit rate for mailings. This is especially helpful for organizations that will do solicitation by mail. Nonprofits are typically exempt from paying property taxes on real estate and other property. Your county assessor's office should be able to give you more information on property or "welfare exemption tax exemption". In addition to property tax exemptions, there are certain exemption benefits from paying income taxes.

Forming a nonprofit corporation is much like creating a regular corporation, except that nonprofits have to take the extra steps of applying for tax-exempt status with the IRS and their state tax division. Many businesses, whether operating as for-profit or nonprofit corporations, partnerships, or sole proprietorships, are required to obtain state or local licenses and permits before commencing business. Here are other things that you may be required to do:

If you plan to hire staff, you may also need to apply for a federal Employer Identification Number (EIN), and apply for your federal and state tax exemptions. You may have to contact the local authorities to find out which licenses and permits may be required for operating your corporation.

Although a nonprofit organization is different from a for-profit organization, you should ascertain with your state department of consumer affairs what you need concerning local business licenses or tax registration certificate for information concerning state licensing requirements for your type of organization. This may be required for your activities. If you plan to sell anything to consumers, you will need a sales tax permit.

You will have to organize and create your corporate bylaws, which spell out the internal and operating rules that govern your nonprofit corporation. Bylaws also contain rules and procedures for holding meetings, voting on issues, and electing directors and officers. You will have to appoint the initial board of directors. This may have to be done before you file your articles, in some states because you have to list their names in the application form. You can follow the instructions and sample in IRS publication 557[39], a self-help resource. Or you can hire a lawyer in your state to draft them for you.

You must also appoint a board of directors and hold a directors' meeting. Typically, the bylaws are adopted by the corporation's directors at their first board meeting. When you hold this first meeting of the board of directors, record the minutes and keep them on file including the agenda, motions carried, and business handled. The board of directors may be made up of one to four individuals that make decisions collectively depending upon the states requirements. Some states have a requirement on the number of members. These board members hold the responsibility and authority to administrate and run the nonprofit corporation.

The main purpose of the first meeting of the board of directors is to conduct the initial business of the corporation. They should handle other formalities such

---

[39] http://www.irs.gov/pub/irs-pdf/p557.pdf,

as recording the receipt of federal and state tax exemptions.

At this meeting, directors should also nominate and elect officers that typically include a president, secretary, and treasurer, which are usually required by state law. In some cases a vice president is required as well. Then, the directors should authorize the newly elected officers to take actions necessary to start the business of the nonprofit which include setting up bank accounts and how the organization will solicit membership. After the completion of the meeting, the minutes of the meeting should be recorded and filed.

In general, a community development corporation will be an organized effort to address an existing problem within a given community. The corporation is modeled after the standard business model, and will attempt to provide services and support that related directly to a current need or problem within a limited geographical area. For more information on exempt organization please go to http://www.irs.gov/charities/index.html.

Use the information provided to assess whether or not your community-focused ministry is ready to serve on a greater level than it is right now by becoming a nonprofit community development organization registered with the Federal government. This status may prove beneficial in a variety of ways to ultimately serve the community at large in a broader way.

BEYOND YOUR DOORS MINISTRY ACTIVATION

Does your ministry have the capacity to create a CDC?

What other partnerships could you form in the community with the creation of a CDC?

Do you understand the difference between providing ministry and a community service? (Please see the Separation of Church and State laws in your area.)

CHAPTER 8

The Caring Community

Many times people in the community become apathetic because they feel so little has been done by the people who have the power to do make the most difference. This indifference is displayed in the attitudes of the people who abuse themselves, because they have lost control of themselves, others and their surroundings. Violence, drugs and prostitution are indicative that people no longer care. They have hit bottom and feel that there is no way out. They give up on trying because they have come to believe that it won't matter.

It is important for organizations to care by providing what is in their power to promote that which is necessary for the health, welfare, maintenance, and protection of the individuals within the community. They also need to display a deep concern and interest in such a way that it is not only expressed but engaging. In order to do this, they must attach importance to the persons or things that need the care." Individuals and organizations can dynamically change this systemic problem systematically by implementing strategies on three levels of caring:

<u>Persons</u> – The primary level of care is to the individual. This is a basic level of personal care that includes programs directed at the promotion of the whole person. It includes a continuing follow-up of ways to support the individual. When individuals feel personally cared for, it builds self-esteem, self-value and self-worth. When a system or organization communicates that it cares, it helps the person feel like a valuable part of the community. The message is clear: "Here is what we want to do to help you to be your best possible self" and then they go about the business of doing what it says. Even though the company may benefit in some way, the person does not feel used or abused in any way. This is why good customer service is so important. Businesses have found that systematized caring makes the difference in the bottom line because people make a psychological shift when they know someone cares and are more likely to cooperate with the agenda.

<u>People</u> –People make up communities. It is the systems within the government, agencies, businesses, and churches that determine how people are cared for in those systems through policies and procedures. This "caring"

has to be systematically intentional. These organizations can run "caring" campaigns by first training and rewarding staff in areas of caring and what that means within their organization. It is important to recognize this level of caring with incentives and awards. When people get recognition from a business, corporation, or agency, it is often considered more valuable than money, and produces a higher rate of productivity. It is important to implement a structure using policies on levels of caring. This may involve revamping and paying more attention to procedures. In order for this system to be effective, caring must become institutionally formalized for duplication, observation, evaluation and fairness.

<u>Place</u> – The tertiary level of care is to the environment. This involves a specialized, highly technical level of advanced diagnostic support services. Specialized personnel are usually trained to address the needs of the population of a larger region and in some cases to the world. But because it is the people who make up the community, when they care and feel cared for, there are reciprocating factors. People understand that they have to give something to get something. They understand this when they care for their own personal spaces but they are limited when it comes the larger environment. When public meeting places and parks are cared for, people have a tendency to be more caring of those places as well as have a greater appreciation for the environment. But

in order for order to be maintained in these areas, there must be parameters set and sometimes even policed.

When looking to create a caring community, it is important that the efforts are systematic. Systematic caring brings about systemic transformation. This requires a reversal of old behaviors and a renewal of established mindsets. This new intentional system requires that the people within the community relearn a new way of being community. This new information is what will bring about revitalization of the community and very possibly a recovery of what has been lost as people reminiscence. The community can even have the potential to experience a renaissance and a new era if they embrace the ethos of caring on every level. The results will produce a renewed sense of optimism within the system that is looking to change.

It is critical to develop and institute a comprehensive plan to target all levels and areas of the community with a strategy of caring. Here are some strategies for a "Caring Community" campaign that can easily be incorporated into any setting or environment with relatively low cost:

<u>People</u> – "Get Caught Caring" photo ops. This idea comes from the nursery school where children get rewards for "being good." Based upon years of results, reward for redirection is a proven strategy that works at getting the desired and changed behaviors.

<u>Place</u> – Rally corporate sponsors for the entire campaign of the visible orientation of the "Caring Community" from lawn signs to public advertising. This can also be advertising opportunities for businesses to get on the "Caring Community" list that residents can in turn frequent with their support. Based upon how much the businesses support the campaign with their resources as well as their behaviors, they can have an opportunity to enter a competition for the top business in the "Caring Community." This is measured by the general public who has the opportunity to vote for them.

An individual neighborhood could hold "We Care Community" events, rallies and get youth involved. This adds another dimension to the typical block party that is often held without a theme that produces community transformation. This could also include talent shows, poster competitions, and an "adopt a school" component and, block clean up events.

Stephen Covey, author of "The 7 Habits of Highly Effective People"[40] encourages us to *"Begin with the end in mind"* This means that you must first consider what you want to see at the conclusion of your process. For most, you would want people to care about themselves as well as their community. An in-depth study should be

---

[40] Covey, Stephen R. *The 7 Habits of Highly Effective People*. New York: Free Press, 2004.

done to appropriately address the current conditions in order to properly assess any problematic systemic issues throughout the community. It is then necessary to create a new system structure and organizational polices that will ultimately override the current system and produce an ethos that includes change behaviors. This system must be so compelling that it infiltrates the psychological mindsets of people to shift to manifest the desired outcomes in the community. The bottom line is that you ultimately want people to care on every level. The focus is to create an environment of caring that inspires people to care. Here are some other ideas for creating a caring community campaign to inspire people to care and create an ethos of caring:

- <u>Advertising</u> - build excitement around the neighborhood about the "We Care Community" which can be advertized on public transportation, business advertising, events to impact all levels of community as well as creates a buy-in, with give-aways, and even involve celebrities.
- <u>Buttons</u> – "iCARE" "I am a part of the We Care Community. This could be the basis for an art-work competition in schools.
- <u>Decals</u> – could introduce the "We Care Community"
- <u>Email</u> – eblasts would build involvement in "We Care Community"

- <u>Newsletters</u> – can give updates on "We Care Community"
- <u>Newspaper articles</u> – to raise awareness and updates the status "We Care Community"
- <u>Posters, street signs</u> - best poster competition can be held in schools about their image of the "We Care Community"
- <u>Radio</u> – examples of how the "We Care Community" is working in the community at large.
- <u>T-Shirts</u> – can be customized with "iCARE" on the front, and "i am a part of the "We Care Community" on the back.
- <u>TV</u> – could give positive highlights of "I am West Center City- I Care" campaign.
- <u>Webinars</u> – could be used to conduct to connect with leaders and participants
- <u>YouTube Videos</u> – could record instances of caring in the "We Care Community" channel, as well as chronicle celebrity appearances

People are always listening to WIIFM ("What's In It For Me?")

The "We Care Community" campaign could offer incentives, rewards, and discounts from businesses (i.e. - 5% discounts for Facebook likes, Twitter sign ups, email addresses, contact info). People could "Win a Wii" – (for the Best Block Competition). The "We Care Community" campaign is win-win situation – everybody wins! Individually and collectively as people care about themselves and what happens in their community and get involved. Leverage resources to reach the goal.

The bottom line is results. Results mean revitalization of the community and systematic change. This will require: the systematic replacement of unhealthy behaviors; a reversal of effects negative influences; residents to relearn a new way of being community: a renewed sense of optimism; the restoration of a sense of purpose; and a Renaissance of a new era for the community.

But the message that the governing agency or organization needs to send to the people is that "We Care" enough to help build your community with the resources it needs to build individual lives. It has been said that *"people don't care how much you know until they know how much you care"*[41]. Before we bombard people with information, facts and even witnessing, we need to first show them how much we care about them as a person with their particular every day basic needs. Then we can create a caring community and practice it within our churches and organizations, and then we can take that same caring out to the place of the lost, dying in a hurting world, where it belongs.

---

[41] Theodore Roosevelt. BrainyQuote.com, Xplore Inc, 2012.
http://www.brainyquote.com/quotes/quotes/t/theodorero140484.html

CHAPTER 9

Opening Up Grant Proposals

Sometimes grant writing can seem like such a huge mystery. There is a system to writing grants that is pretty consistent throughout regardless of what arena that you are in. If you learn the basics, it could become simple to understand. What is most important is that you know how to follow instructions...to a tee. Try not to veer too far off course of what you are being asked to respond to a question in a proposal. This is not the place for too much creativity. Try to stick pretty close to a direct response to the questions asked. You are often graded as to whether or not you answered the questions correctly and also on how thoroughly you answered. Below are parts of a proposal that you may encounter and may be included in most Request for Proposals (RFP) or Requests for Application (RFA).

Abstract

An abstract is a brief summary of the proposed plan. It includes a description of the community to be served, the estimated number of participants, any partners, the outcomes and goals, as well as the activities that will be involved. This is typically meant to be concise with no more than 500 words. You should begin with a statement of the problem that you are attempting to solve and why you feel motivated and qualified to do so. You want to state your methodology for going about to solve the predicament based upon how you are going to go about your work to get the intended outcomes. It is important to include any research that you have done to bring you to your conclusions as well as how you came up with the best practices as your plan of action. You can end with what you believe can be accomplished given the data. Close with the change that you believe will come about as a result of your work.

Needs Assessment

A needs assessment is a description that includes an evaluation of the needs of the population that you intend to serve and includes available resources. It also includes a plan of action of how you intend to meet those needs. This is generally a systematic process that provides a snapshot of the current conditions and helps to determine priorities of need. It is a process that collects and evaluates information and then utilizes quantitative and qualitative data that is relevant to the program to develop a plan of action. All persons involved should be a part of the needs assessment and building the strategic plan.

You will be required to present demographical information regarding age, grade, ethnicity, gender, economic household and employment information. You can get this information from the census. General information gathering is often done using surveys of various kinds that are designed to get the specific information needed. You have to both collect and analyze the data to substantiate your objectives. This data will also be used to measure your effectiveness so be careful not to exaggerate the numbers and skew the outcomes. You will also want to assess the beliefs, opinion and attitude of those who you which to serve to better understand their perceived need. This can be accomplished through questionnaires, surveys, interviews and detailed observation of behaviors.

Application Information

This is general information needed about your organization which includes your legal organization's name, complete address and telephone number and includes a lead contact person or persons. Be sure to add this information correctly and be sure to include working phone numbers. You may also be asked for a web address.

Grant Amounts

Often the grant amount is an open number between a minimum and a maximum. Other times the amount of the grant is based upon your capacity to deliver service which is determined by the funding organization. Grant amounts can often be paid on a reimbursement basis. This means that you have to spend the money before you get the money. This can often be difficult for grassroots organizations. When grants are structured this way, you will more than likely get an advance to get you started. This advance will be incrementally deducted every time you submit an invoice until the balance is paid in full.

Location

There is a difference between where you conduct your business and where your proposed programs will be held. If these are both the same location, then you would simply put the same location down twice. But if your business office is different from where you will implement your programming then you need to be able to provide both addresses. Try to avoid using a post office box unless you specify that it is a mailing address only.

Partners

Few grantors are apt to distribute funding to solitary organizations. They are more likely to give money to a group or a collaborative of organizations. The logic is that the more people involved, the more likely the project will get off the ground and succeed. You must be prepared to identify all partners that will be included in the grant proposal as well as the key roles that they will play. You may also be asked to provide letters of endorsement from each organization that you mention in order to be considered for funding. Proposal partnerships can take on many forms. Some may be financial partners and bear the cost of the program service delivery while others have no financial obligation but provide donations in-kind through materials, supplies, or administrative services.

Program Summary

Next, you will be asked to summarize the type of your proposed program. If you are proposing to run a program at more than one site, you may have to complete an application for each site. In other cases, you may need to fill out a certain section of the proposal application with the information for each site. This summary should include the activity that you plan to provide, the days and times in the week and your beginning and starting times. You may also be required to add the number of staffing that will facilitate the program in addition to their qualifications.

To start, you should begin with your program highlights and successes. This is a good place to promote your history of community service and your effectiveness.

Often churches don't realize that much of the work that they do is a benefit to the community like food drives or even helping children to read in Sunday School. Take a close analysis of your ministry work and build your base of community effectiveness. See everything you do as a service to the community for this is in fact what it is. This is also a good place to talk about any current or anticipated challenges that you face. This presents your program proposal in a realistic light. Be sure to discuss how you plan to overcome your obstacles and address your challenges. Always leave your funder with a positive assurance about your strategy to accomplish your outcomes.

You should also discuss how many participants that you plan to serve and how you plan to recruit and retain them in your program. Outline your strategy and the results that you foresee in a particular timeframe. Also anticipate the challenges you may have in getting participants in the program and have a plan to address those as well.

Most funders have guidelines for quality. You should be thoroughly aware of these guidelines and be prepared to address how you will meet them in your proposal based upon the funder's contract requirements. Be sure that you set realistic goals and then can carry out the goals that you set.

You may also be asked to provide a detailed program description delineating the goals and objectives that you created based upon the needs assessment and how you anticipate fostering a change in behavior based upon your program model which aligns with the grant's desired outcomes.

Something else to consider is to specifically describe how you plan to administer the service in a way that improves the quality of life for those that you intend to serve and the long term effects that this will have on the participants and the community. This helps funders to feel comfortable about giving you money. It is important to say something that speaks to your tenure and your ability to sustain the program for a lasting period of time so that they can feel that their money has been wisely invested.

Professional Development Plan

In order to effectively run a program where staff is clear on accomplishing the goals and objectives it is necessary to provide ongoing staff training either on or off the site of your program. You may need to send you staff to a training facility or you can bring trainers you're your program site. You cannot assume that everyone you hire will catch the vision. You must be able to describe your plan for professional development that will be provided to your staff and you must also show how these trainings will advance your staff's knowledge of how to address the area of need. Discuss the types of training as well as the qualifications of those who will provide the training thoroughly. Finally, you should also demonstrate how the training relates to assisting in accomplishing the desired outcomes.

Program Evaluation

There are times when the funder wants to know how you plan to evaluate your program. This can be done by the individual program with satisfaction surveys, or interviews. A pre- and a post-test can also determine how well the program succeeded at its goals based upon the participant's knowledge or status before the program and then once a particular timeframe of the program is complete. If you are using an independent evaluator, you will have to provide sufficient background information on the evaluator and their qualifications in the field as well as how they will go about conducting the professional evaluation. You should be able to state the measures that will be used in the evaluation using indicators that will help to determine what needs to be and what has been achieved using qualitative and quantitative measures for performance. In order to effectively evaluate any program, the data needed must be collected and review periodically in a time sequence and a quantity that must be stated. You should also describe how the data will be analyzed and the purpose it will be used once it has been analyzed.

Performance Measures

In order to determine how effective your program was at solving the identified problem, you must use performance measured and indicators that will determine how well the program worked. This is typically stated in a percentage of the population making the proposed achievement in a particular area. For example, if you are teaching about home ownership to a group of single parents, you could say that "70% of the participants will obtain a greater knowledge in the area of how to apply for a mortgage". Your performance will be proved by pre- and a post-test results.

Collaboration/Coordination

As stated earlier, funders are more likely to fund a group or collaboration because there are more people involved that are interested in the success of the program's outcomes. You must describe just how the proposed program structure will function at leveraging resources from all parties involved. You also want to state how the provision of services will be coordinated with each organization and who is responsible for what, when and where.

This may also include the development of an advisory board that governs the partnership which each person on the board having duties and responsibilities that help the program implementation, operation, evaluation run smoothly. You want to include the frequency and times of meetings that are planned along with the primary persons responsible for administrating the various tasks needed to run the collaborative and the program.

Sustainability

It is one thing to receive funding and yet another thing to be able to sustain a program after funding has ended. You should be able to verbalize a strategic plan for securing funding well after the funding has ended. This would include everything various fundraising activities to soliciting other organizations to make substantial contributions to the work on an on-going bases.

Budget

Creating a budget is just as important as providing a community service. If you do not have enough funding to run a program, you may not be able to achieve your objectives which can be very frustrating. Be sure that you prepare a complete budget that includes all of the necessary costs of the program operation even if these things are going to be donated. A non-profit budget typically includes line items that involve staffing, benefits, materials and supplies in addition to rent, utilities, telephone, maintenance, transportation and training. Office supplies, printing, advertising, meals, postage, and security are some additional costs. Other items could include administrative costs that are often hidden or buried such as security clearances, licenses, professional and technical services and legal fees as well as fees charged by your bank and credit cards.

Closing the Proposal

Once you understand the parts of a proposal, you are in a good position to successfully write a proposal that clearly and thoroughly state how you are qualified to address the needs in your community. These types of grants are sure to be funded by any organization that is interested in investing their money in community transformation. Organizations that have the ability to provide funding are evidently prospering and see it is their way to give back. But remember that these donations come with a price and you have to do your homework if you are going to be successful at receiving it.

You have to also be prepared to report your progress both financially and logistically. There are some grants that include a built in monitoring process that actually include a staff person that comes to your site to observe your progress in the provision of services. In most cases, these persons are there as an asset to your program and are interested in your success.

Lastly, because the church is in the community, it is in the most advantageous position to do the most good to meet the needs of the neighborhood. Most important-ly, if you ever have the opportunity to write a grant for funding, you should never underestimate the power of prayer. You need to pray and ask God for wisdom and guidance in the beginning of the grant writing process. Ask God if this is something that you should be doing and how to go about the implementation process. This way, you can rest assured that you will fulfill your call to "go out into all the world"… past your doors and make a difference right where you are…and beyond.

CHAPTER 10

Ministering to the Monsters

During the course of writing this book I had a dream. I am not sure exactly the context but what I do remember was a grossly disfigured creature, with a huge head, standing at a set of double doors peering out. Standing next to the creature was a minister who was ever so gently encouraging the creature to take the risk and go beyond the doors with a very assuring tone that it was possible. Gripped with fear, the disfigured creature refused to believe that it was feasible. There was also another character nearby that was as sneaky as it was seductive.

Many would consider the disfigured ogre in the dream to be a monster. If I could be so bold as to interpret the dream I would say that the grossly disfigured creature in the dream is the Church. The huge head represents the fact that the church is so preoccupied with itself and so absorbed within itself that it has become a disfiguration from what it was originally intended to become. This huge head is also the symbol of the self-centeredness of the Church to be so focused upon its own affairs that it cannot dream of doing anything else but caring for itself, nurturing itself and protecting itself.

To make matters worse the disfigured creature is afraid to go past the door because it cannot fathom a new reality. But this fear is self inflicted because the minister was trying to convince the creature of the fact that there is a whole world beyond the door that is filled with rich potential and promise. The minister at the door is the Holy Spirit. The Holy Spirit is ever so gently encouraging us to go beyond our doors to get everything that is needed for wholeness and reconciliation. The huge monster of the church is the fear of rejection. Sometimes the Church is afraid to begin the process because of the fear of ridicule. People refuse to fulfill the Great Commission[42] because they are afraid of being rejected by the same world that needs to hear the restoring message of the Gospel of Jesus Christ. This paradox is intensified by the seductive character whose deceptive spirit lulls us into believing that it is safer and more pleasurable to be self seeking and self gratifying…inside the doors.

---

[42] Matthew 28:16-2

But as tempting as this is for the church, it is critical that the Church resists the posture of pleasure-seeking and commit to seek to please the One that we are called to serve. I remember being an observer in the dream. I remember how sorry I felt for the creature that just could not see the possibilities and even refused to see beyond its own circumstances. I also specifically remember the sensation of being distracted by the seductive character whose tried to maintain the focus on selfish, self-centered activities. What was also important to note was that the seductive character was so cunning it was almost unnoticeable because it had become a familiar part of the scenery. But isn't that how satan works to deceive us— with something that is familiar. It is the familiar that causes us to lower our resistance as well as let down our guard.

But if the church will fulfill its mission, it must minister to the monster of fear that keeps the church from fulfilling its vision. As we particularly attend to what ails us, we can then care for others more appropriately as outlined by Christ. It is when we face with our own monsters that we can better deal with the monsters that we face in society. But it is only when we face the reality that the monster is us that we can more effectively serve and fulfill the mission of comforting the world with the love of Jesus Christ.

When we take the time to address and recognize what is prone to seducing us, we can come out of denial and move past it. Then we can begin the work of doing real ministry. Although the feat seems monstrous, Jesus is there to help us. God would not ask us to do anything that we did not have the capacity to do. And when we remember that we are bound by the commands of Jesus, then we should be compelled to do whatever it takes to make it happen. Then we will be able to do so without offering creative excuses of convenience.

And if we are afraid, we must be honest about the root of our fears. We must recognize that our fears are misdirected. The bible says that the fear of the Lord is the beginning of wisdom.[43] If we are to fear anything, it is God but not with a dreadful sensation but with an overwhelming sense of reverence and awe. When we fear God this way, we are inspired to serve out of a sense of reverential accountability. In her book "Ministry at the Margins: The Prophetic Mission of Women, Youth and the Poor" (Sanders 1997), Dr. Cheryl Sanders sums it up this way:

> *"The fear of the Lord is the beginning of wisdom because it gives us a good reason for choosing what is right and provides a clear rationale for repentance when we are wrong. Many people don't care about making right choices because they don't give a thought to who God is and what is God's will. But*

---

[43] Proverbs 9:10

*God-fearing people choose the good because we know
we are accountable to God.*[44]

We saw in an earlier chapter that a lot of what we
should do to help others centers around helping "the
least of these." And there are so many that fit into this
category that we can hardly report a shortage. It is no
secret that women and children make up the population
as being the most poor. These statistics are true all over
the world. The reasons for this disparity center around
issues of sexism, classism, racism and exploitation. These
statistics make women and children easy targets for
community centered ministry opportunities—the
possibilities are endless.

But Dr. Sanders helps us to put things in perspective
when she states:

*"The promise of eternal life is given to those who
give the Kingdom Mandate priority in earthly life.
The parable urges us to discern the face of Christ in
the faces of human suffering."*

She also confirms with clarity what Jesus has made
clear: that it is our response to these faces of human
suffering that is the real test for us. These faces have

---

[44] Sanders, Cheryl J. Ministry At The Margins: The Prophetic
Mission to Women, Youth and the Poor. InterVarsity, Downers
Grove, Illinois, 1997. P.23

heads but they are not necessarily "big" heads. They are normal everyday heads that we see in the faces of the people in our community in every place we are. When we are honest, this is doable and the task is not as daunting. As we minister to our own monsters, we are better able to conquer the fear that keeps us from seeing these faces.

In the end all that really matters is that we get our priorities straight and do those things that advance the Kingdom of God. Dr. Sanders sums it up this way, and I will close with this:

> *"A ministry that employs God's resources to meet human need is never a dry and dead work, but instead is exciting and exhilarating evidence that the Kingdom is at hand. It is time for Christians everywhere to reconsider this Kingdom Mandate to serve the needs of the present age as both recipients and reciprocators of God's promise. The absolute prerequisite of the promise of life is to honor life in the here and now with compassion. For we cannot embrace God's promise of life in eternity without respecting God's gift of life in the "least of these."* [45]

Need I say more?

---

[45] Ibid. p. 34

Bibliography

Bakke, Ray. *A Theology As Big As The City*. Downers Grove, Illinois: InterVarsity Press, 1997.

Covey, Stephen R. *The 7 Habits of Highly Effective People*. New York: Free Press, 2004.

Center for Applied Research. Nike's *"Just Do It"* Advertising Campaign.
http://www.cfar.com/Documents/nikecmp.pdf.

Dr. George Barna, *"Leadership Secrets for Cutting Edge Distinction"* (lecture, May 31, 2010, Milwaukee, WI).

Hartford Institute for Religion Research.
http://hirr.hartsem.edu/research/fastfacts/fast_facts.html#sizecong

Kupcha-Szrom, Jaclyn. *"Early Language and Literacy Development."* Zero To Three.
http://www.zerotothree.org/public-policy/policy-toolkit/early-literacywebmarch1-6.pdf.

ProLiteracy America. *"U.S. Adult Literacy Programs: Making a Difference."* Accessed April 2, 2012.
http://www.proliteracy.org/NetCommunity/Document.Doc?id=18.

Roosevelt, Theodore. BrainyQuote.com, Xplore Inc, 2012.
http://www.brainyquote.com/quotes/quotes/t/theodorero
140484.html

Sanders, Chery J. *Ministry at the Margins: The Prophetic Mission of Women, Youth & the Poor.* Downers Grove, Illinois: InterVarsity Press, 1997.

Spanglish (2004). Box Office Mojo.
http://www.boxofficemojo.com/movies/?id=spanglish.htm
Retrieved August 30, 2009.

Index

ORGANIZATIONAL S.W.O.T.

ORGANIZATIONAL STRENGTHS

Advantages	
Experiences, Knowledge	
Unique Characteristics	
Resources	
Geographical Advantage Location	
Competence, Capabilities	
Reputation	

Comments:

ORGANIZATIONAL S.W.O.T. (Cont'd.)

ORGANIZATIONAL WEAKNESSES
(Inside the organization)

Disadvantages	
Experiences and Knowledge Gap	
Lack of liability, Trust	
Lack of Resources	
Geographical Challenges Location	
Loss of competent capable staff	
Loss or lack of reputation	

Comments:

ORGANIZATIONAL S.W.O.T. (Cont'd.)

ORGANIZATIONAL OPPORTUNITIES

Strategic Alliances, Partnerships	
Innovation	
Unique Selling Point (U.S.P.)	

Comments:

ORGANIZATIONAL THREATS

(Outside the organization)

Loss of alliances and partnerships	
Strong competition	
Saturated market	

Comments:

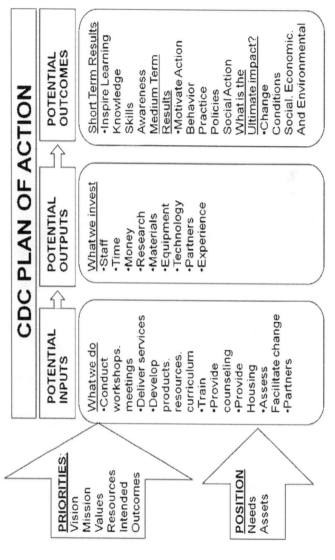

CDC PLAN OF ACTION

POTENTIAL INPUTS

POTENTIAL OUTPUTS

POTENTIAL OUTCOMES

What we do
- Conduct workshops. meetings
- Deliver services
- Develop products. resources. curriculum
- Train
- Provide counseling
- Provide Housing
- Assess
- Facilitate change
- Partners

What we invest
- Staff
- Time
- Money
- Research
- Materials
- Equipment
- Technology
- Partners
- Experience

Short Term Results
- Inspire Learning Knowledge Skills Awareness

Medium Term Results
- Motivate Action Behavior Practice Policies Social Action

What is the Ultimate impact?
- Change Conditions Social. Economic. And Environmental

PRIORITIES:
Vision
Mission
Values
Resources
Intended Outcomes

POSITION
Needs
Assets

Figure 1

About the Author

Dr. LaVerne Adams is an author, certified life coach and inspirational speaker. She specializes in coaching celebrities and high powered professionals in need of spiritual guidance and emotional support. She is passionate about sharing her wisdom from years of experience and training to help people to define their destiny, maximize their potential and live the life of their dreams.

The Reverend Dr. LaVerne Adams celebrates over 15 years as Pastor, Teacher, and Vision Architect of the Cathedral of Praise Community Church which began in 1997 and is located in the Overbrook section of West Philadelphia, Pennsylvania. Today the Church is thriving with vibrant worship and countless community outreach programs to youth, which is the signature of this growing ministry. Her leadership has helped the church to transform its community, develop disciples and prepare leaders in the Kingdom of God. She is a recognized church leader with the American Baptist Churches, USA and is a member of the Abundant Harvest Fellowship of

Churches under the leadership of Bishop David Evans. She has served as an advisor to many great people.

As Executive Director, she has developed educational outreach programs at the church's 30,000 square-foot campus. They minister to over 100 families in the community daily through the Motivational Achievement Program (MAP), a before- and after-school program, which continues into a full-day Techno Arts Summer Camp specializing in the arts, media, and technology. Additionally, The Cathedral Learning Center is a full-service preschool, with a curriculum that is literacy-based and includes the "I Can Read Program" to inspire infants to preschoolers to have a long-lasting love for reading. These programs employ over 20 people from the community.

As community leader, Dr. Adams has been awarded Community Service Awards by Mayor Michael Nutter, State Representative Louise Williams Bishop, and State Senator Vincent Hughes. She has also been awarded numerous federal, state, city, and private grants to continue her work in the community. Continued efforts are being made to provide relevant opportunities to community residents; turning this once deteriorating neighborhood into a place "where God lives in the Praise" (Psalm 22:3).

As professor, Dr. Adams is a graduate of Palmer Theological Seminary with a Doctor of Ministry degree which focused on the Renewal of the Church for Mission and the holistic needs of youth in church and community. She was nominated for "Who's Who in American Universities" in 1996. Since 1998, she has served as professor at the Eastern School of Christian ministry and adjunct faculty of Palmer Seminary teaching courses in Community-Focused Ministry, Stewardship, and Small Group Ministry. Dr. Adams has also taught Bible and Foundations for Christian Spirituality at Eastern University's Esperanza College.

As author, she has written "Destiny: By Divine Design" and "Driven By Destiny" with the foreword written by Dr. Rick Warren, to help many discover their true destiny by proactively participating in destiny dialogs designed to maximize their potential. As Inspirational Life Coach she is affectionately known as "The Doctor of Destiny™" and is life coach to celebrities and high-powered professionals in need of spiritual guidance and affirmation. As she encourages victory in every situation, She is affectionately known as Dr. V. She was co-host of the "Single, Saved & Satisfied" radio broadcast with "Dezzie" on Praise 103.9FM. She has also been featured for her zest for life in *The Philadelphia Tribune* and *Redbook* magazine, as well as other local papers. Dr. Adams has even been seen on Fox Television along with her triplet sisters. She is host to the "*Your Date With Destiny*" life-changing events that dynamically transforms participants to shift into their destiny. The inaugural event, held on 10-10-10, included Tasha Smith, from

Tyler Perry's movie "*Why Did I Get Married, Too?*" and was a stellar success transforming the lives of all in attendance. Dr. Adams is also a songwriter with songs like "*Our Wedding Day*", "*Love's Not Blind*", "*I Know*", "*Ready or Not*", and "*I Wanna Be With You*", which speaks to the heart of what it means to be human and spiritually alive.

As dynamic preacher, teacher, and transformational speaker, she believes that her God-given calling is to make God truly known to every person she encounters.

As scholar practitioner, Dr. Adams is the recent recipient of the Lilly Endowment National Clergy Renewal Program award. Dr. Adams had the opportunity to hone her Spanish-language skills through lengthy sojourns in Latin America with the expressed purpose to learn the language and the culture in order to minister more effectively to a multicultural audience. She traveled to Port of Spain, Trinidad, Venezuela, Mexico, Dominican Republic, Costa Rica and Puerto Rico.

As ambassador, Dr. Adams has world-wide influence and has been launched to the nations, traveling internationally spreading the holistic gospel of Jesus Christ to the Americas, Africa, India, the Caribbean, and the Philippines. She is host to the Christian Women's International Empowerment Conference launched in Bridgetown, Barbados, West Indies and is scheduled to span locations around the globe. It is her personal mission is to develop a relationship with God that is so authentically transformational that it compels multitudes to do likewise.

For more information and speaking engagements contact:

Cathedral of Praise Community Church and
International Kingdom Strategy Center
6400 Haverford Avenue
Philadelphia, PA 19151
215.474.2680 phone • 215.474.7586 fax
DoctorofDestiny@aol.com
www.TheDoctorOfDestiny.com™
www.CathedralofPraiseInternational.org

DRIVE YOUR DESTINY
Driven By Destiny
Mini-Book Series

PART I: REDESIGN YOUR LIFE

Volume 1. The Secret Key to Review Your Life -
"Start With the Frame"

This is your opportunity to take a good look at your life and to determine what you see as its themes, purpose, and dreams. Think about where you are and where you want to be. Prepare for the journey of a lifetime!

Volume 2. The Secret Key to Your Rediscovery -
"What's Under the Hood?"

Think about whether or not your current experiences broaden or limit you. Now think about all of the adverse circumstances in your life. Expand your thinking to the possibility that these situations exist to help you discover something wonderful about yourself . . . that you never imagined before. Get ready to make some new discoveries!

Volume 3. The Secret Key to Your Revelation -
"Available Options"

Think about the last time God revealed something to you. Think about the way that God may have spoken to you that you may have missed. Was it in a still small voice or through another person? Now, think about ways that you could position yourself to hear from God about your future. Be prepared for many things will be revealed to you now!

Volume 4. The Secret Key to Your Renewal- "Remanufactured"

As you come to this dimension you will think about your lifestyle habits and how long you may have had them. Next, you will think about the process by which these habits may have developed. Now, think about ways you can develop new disciplines that can strengthen and bring a renewal in your life. Get ready for a spring of refreshing living waters bursting forth to wash away all the stagnant waters!

PART II: REALIGN YOUR LIFE

Volume 5. The Secret Key to Your Reinvention - "It Had to Be Totalled!"

Take this moment and think about the last time you changed something in your life. Think about what the change felt like and the process involved. Now imagine changes in your character, outlook, or appearance that could make your life soar. Now, get ready for a total makeover. You will be inspired to transform. You are about to be transformed in ways you never imagined!

Volume 6. The Secret Key to Your Responsibility - "Have Car, Will Travel"

As you approach this dimension, begin to think about the level of opportunities currently available in your life. Think about how well positioned you are for advancement or success. Think about what obstacles might be in the way of your destiny opportunities. Now, imagine how far you could advance if all conditions were favorable for you to reach your goals. Get ready! You are about to drive your way to the opportunity of a lifetime.

Volume 7. The Secret Key to Your Reason - "The Power of Dreams"

Take the opportunity to think about your reason for being alive. Think about what God's intended desire was for your life when God created you. Now, think about your goals, dreams, and desires. Determine that you will fulfill every purpose God intended and that you will stop at nothing until you are driven by your passion!

Volume 8. The Secret Key to Your Relationships -
"Making Electric Connections"

Think deeply about the connections and associations in your life. Think about whether or not those relationships add to or subtract from you. Determine whether they encourage you on your journey toward your destiny. Now imagine how refreshing a mutually loving, caring relationship could be. Get ready to make covenant connections and walk in covenant agreement for your destiny!

PART III - REGENERATE YOUR LIFE

Volume 9. The Secret Key to Your Results -
"The Vehicle of the Future"

Think about your close and distant future. Think about some of the things you would like to see happen in your life in one, three, and five year periods. Now imagine what you would need in order for you to see your future success. Move forward in your destiny and begin to drive your dreams!

Volume 10. The Secret Key to Your Reflection -
"Feel the Difference"

Think about what you might be looking forward to in your life. Think about the probability of these things happening. Now, raise your level of anticipation and expect the unexpected! Don't just dream it, drive it and create a higher standard!

Think about a time that you may have experienced a miracle, no matter how insignificant you think it might have been. Think about a time that God did something in your life that you knew was out of the ordinary or defied natural laws. Now imagine that you believe that you can have experiences every day that leave you in awe and wonder. Get ready for a miracle and the drive of your life!

Volume 12. *The Secret Key to Your Reward -* *"Travel Well"*

Think about the things in your life that make you more aware that you have a very unique destiny. Think about the course of events and themes that help you better understand the special direction for your life. You will begin see more clearly the greatness of your inevitable future. Now walk right into your destiny as you define your destiny, maximize your potential to live the life of your dreams.

Driven By Destiny:
12 Secret Keys to Unlock Your Future

Driven By Destiny Discovery Manual E-book
&
Driven By Destiny 30 Day Devotional E-book

You can get your download copy of these
valuable resources free with your
Driven By Destiny
Proof of Purchase
Please email DoctorOfDestiny@aol.com
And include your place of purchase and receipt #.

COMING SOON!

To help you on your
your destiny journey …

Driven By Destiny in Spanish
De la Mano del Destino

Also, COMING SOON the new
Driven By Destiny Journal
and the
Driven By Destiny Bible

For more information please go to:
www.DrivenByDestiny.com

Please friend Dr. LaVerne Adams

on Facebook

For your Daily Dose of Destiny

Made in the USA
Charleston, SC
24 May 2012